FORKED TONGUE

Books by W.N. Herbert

POETRY

Sterts & Stobies, with Robert Crawford (Obog Books, 1985)
Sharawaggi, with Robert Crawford (Polygon, 1990)
The Landfish (Duncan of Jordanstone College of Art, 1991)
Dundee Doldrums (Galliard, 1991)
Anither Music (Vennel Press, 1991)
The Testament of the Reverend Thomas Dick (Arc Publications, 1994)
Forked Tongue (Bloodaxe Books, 1994)

LITERARY CRITICISM

To Circumjack MacDiarmid (Oxford University Press, 1992)

FORKED TONGUE

W.N. HERBERT

BLOODAXE BOOKS

ISBN: 1 85224 267 1

First published 1994 by
Bloodaxe Books Ltd,
P.O. Box 1SN,
Newcastle upon Tyne NE99 1SN.

Bloodaxe Books Ltd acknowledges
the financial assistance of Northern Arts.

Cover printing by J. Thomson Colour Printers Ltd, Glasgow.

Printed in Great Britain by
Bell & Bain Limited, Glasgow, Scotland.

Acknowledgements

THE CORTINA SONATA
Parts of *The Cortina Sonata* have appeared in the anthologies *Dream State: The New Scottish Poetry*, edited by Donny O'Rourke (Polygon, 1994), *Other Tongues*, edited by Robert Crawford (Verse Publications, 1990) and *New Writing Scotland*, edited by Edwin Morgan & Christopher Whyte (Association for Scottish Literary Studies, 1987-89) as well as in *Poetry Review* and *Verse*.

THE LANDFISH
Some of these poems have appeared in *Agenda, Angel Exhaust, Cencrastus, Chapman, Gairfish, Northwords, Verse* and *Zed 2 Oh*. Some appeared in the anthologies *The New Poetry*, edited by Michael Hulse, David Kennedy and David Morley (Bloodaxe Books, 1993), *The New Makars*, edited by Tom Hubbard (Mercat Press, 1991), *Other Tongues*, and *Poetry with an Edge*, edited by Neil Astley (Bloodaxe Books, new edition, 1993). 'The Landfish' was first published in a limited edition pamphlet by Duncan of Jordanstone Art College, Dundee, in 1991. 'Hawthornden Morning Blues' and 'To a Fly' were written during a Fellowship at Hawthornden Castle.

TICKA TICKA
'A Temporal Ode' appeared in *The Wide Skirt*.

OMNEGADDRUMS
These poems were first collected in the pamphlets *Dundee Doldrums* (Galliard, Edinburgh, 1991), *Sterts & Stobies*, with Robert Crawford (Obog Books, Oxford, 1985), *Sharawaggi*, with Robert Crawford (Polygon, Edinburgh, 1991) and *Anither Music* (Vennel Press, London, 1991). Some have appeared in the anthologies *Dream State: The New Scottish Poetry, The Faber Book of Twentieth-Century Scottish Poetry*, edited by Douglas Dunn (Faber, 1992), *The New Poetry*, and *Poetry with an Edge*, as well as in a number of magazines. 'Weather Forecast' was broadcast on STV as part of the programme *New Acquaintance* in January 1992.

The prefatory note, *I Tell a Lie*, was commissioned by the Poetry Book Society for their Bulletin.

Contents

I TELL A LIE

When my grandmother makes a mistake she says 'Eh tell a leh'. Maybe it's the Calvin in her makes her confess to lying when she isn't. But I feel the same whenever I use conversational English picked up after fourteen years in Oxford. Or whenever I lapse into a full-throated Dundonian Scots at home and someone announces, *'Ye've no lost yir accent'*. Herbert speak with forked tongue.

One strand wiggles back to Blackness Primary and recites *'Yir heid's daft, / Yir belly's saft, / An yir bum is medd o leathir'*. The other coils around Brasenose College and dreams of Marius the Epicurean. But I don't want to choose between them; I want both prongs of the fork. Aren't we continually hopping registers like socially-challenged crickets? My motto is: *And not Or*. This is what links *Landfish*, which is in Scots, to *The Cortina Sonata*, which is about Scottishness.

For the *Sonata* I wanted a structure that bound themes together without blurring their distinctness, and found it in the classical sonata, which elaborates on two separate ideas, modulating them from major to minor, and so on. My themes were: my upbringing, and my experience of foreignness. So I talk about my grandfather's love of flowers in one breath, and a Renaissance courtier in Florence in the next. By looking at both the outside and the inside of my Scottishness, I hope to arrive at some melodious conclusions.

Landfish could have been a kind of New Demotic verse; boiling the idiolect down to something I'm able to say in a pub. But that would be a poetry that's afraid of getting beaten up. Most of my Scots, to be blunt, gets the shit kicked out of it. I don't stay "true" to how *thi Peopul* speak: I search dictionaries for gorgeous defunct fragments; I make things up. I think that's the poet's task: to invent new ways of saying that are beautiful even after they've had the shit kicked out of them. So *Landfish* is peculiar, baroque. It may be a challenge to read, but that's the challenge: come on in, the clytach's lovely.

Then there's *Ticka Ticka*, which is about a certain industrial dispute. I spent my teenage summers "working" in Dundee's Timex factories. My father worked there for thirty years, as did many of his friends, at managerial and shopfloor levels. Last year's strike was deeply divisive of this community, and the final, inevitable closure left a bitter aftertaste of impotence. *Ticka Ticka* combines personal memory and voices from Dundee's radical past to try and make some sense of these events. It's not a politically correct piece of polemic, it's an attempt to heal the division this dispute opened in me.

The last section is called *Omnegaddrums*, which my dictionary defines as 'a miscellaneous collection, a medley, the unincorporated craftsmen of the burgh'.

THE CORTINA SONATA

'As well as the styling and the light body, it wasn't called something boring like an Oxford or a Cambridge. Its name evoked feelings of a spirit of adventure. It was like a holiday every time you got into it.'

— ANDY THORN, *Cortina driver*

I: ANDANTE CON MOTOR: *PIBROCH*

*One of these little sphinxes of the air was washing himself. How fast
a threatened fly departs! The decision is instantaneous and there
seems to be no inertia to overcome and there is no superfluity in the
way flies take off.*

SAUL BELLOW

In Morning
(for Thomas Neil)

A small, bay-windowed room, badly emulsioned white;
the garden is carefully held, beyond it, by dawn.
Pink stains the Michaelmas daisies and
the tough, shrugging backs of overgrown spinach leaves
draw into dew-filled wrinkles with
                              a fatigue of stretching.
Coarse grey brushstrokes with the hairs embedded
coat the walls with horse, and flies,
flies everywhere, ill-mannered stops.

Out there, beyond the ivy's tendril-
coiling arch, is a glass of Renaissance air, cupped
by a memory of the tread through long grass
like a hand. Gloved in day's colours, where
a primaveran coolness clings
                              to the youngest shadows,
the hand touches a *bocca di leone*, or, snapdragon, or,
to my grandfather, a 'barkin doaggie': it has
a wattle-fleered jaw, clamped resolutely in
weak crimson; it has
a courtier's complexion, and is as many-titled as those
that decked the streets of Florence.

In here, at the steam-filled, filling sink, the smell
is nearly of peat-water, the hand collides with china,
becoming a scratched bath, into which, long since,
brown leaves have shredded. A glittering dark liquid

is distilled, of funerary voices
discussing flowers...voices thumb over
quartz and granite in the memory,
jumbling, to make an *uisgebeatha*
                                none can replicate.

Between such worlds, the only commerce is
a fly, a bundle of germs, quite irrational in
its landings and leavings. And the bulby spider, a
brownspeckled egg, with legs translucently banded,
a dyed hand,
strung out on its almost-map, imposes
its own embargo.
It doesn't stray from the weave's skeletal city; flies
may even pass beneath its strands,
walking on the windowpane,
half-searching for a hole in the nothingness
that nonetheless contains them; but in its domain
it all-devours, lump
by bolted lump.
                        What are our exiles between? The hand
produces nothing by its own design
that does not separate, cell by cell,
this consciousness from one embrace.

Yet all these echoes of that rebirth are
seen through this umber curtain of his fragrant mould,
as though between the blindfold of brown fingers:
there must be a hole in the nothingness that
only such architecture can reveal.

A Hothouse Effect

How much of the real are you
prepared to let past you? It was
raining, and Craig Raine was

behind us as we went into the second
hothouse, enquiring vigorously into
what's not Latin name. No comment,

the day gave me this instant,
as particular as the melody
of names unsonorously said, whose

meanings may no longer reach
my big ignorant nose, thrust bewildered at
transistorised narcissi,

Fernandesii; attached to the yellow moustache
of *Puschkinia Libanotica*, dying in
its own blue snow; offended by

a favourite cypress being *Lawsoniana*,
'Ellwood's pillar': why? You are in a green-
house with your mother, gaping at

green elephant flaps, mouse-fast fish;
her fingers are on all the petals but
break none, like strange beaks. You both

laugh at *Whitfieldia Lateritia*: Dundee's slum
is Oxford's exotica. You both pace round
an intense earth of coffee, date, orange, lime:

in this vegetable world it is
as though no reason for distance
could find root. In ten minutes she'll

touch a painted saint's petal nose, on camera,
in an hour complain over-vigorously of
Assam in Rosie Lee's, and I will see

nothing but *Strelitzae Reginae*,
the orange jackal ears emerging from
a red frost muzzle, and the purple bird

that burst from its brows, 'wee
riots' of them as I said at once, in-
voluntarily in my own tongue.

I have my grandfather's hands
and she their greenness; I left her
no other room to be gentle in but out

of doors, and there it seems an ease
of starlings, seizing life. I go home
accompanied by my vision. I see

Eranthemum Pulchellum in blue water-
pistol, shoehorn, fork; I see *Euphorbia
Globosa* as potatoes inspired by Miró.

I find a daffodil broken like a pencil
and take it to brighten up my room
with its dying. I see *Platycerium*

Calcicorne, a wood fibrous bowl tied to
its sample bark, transforming mould and
withering to a beautiful skeleton

its inner skin.

Mnemonic Entomica

Sometimes it's hard to wait for time
to make the links between its elements,

even though they may not be from
the same chain, in the way a list

imposes its uneven causalities,
individual as a spine you find

your hand is working on instead of
stroking. In the photo you hold me

mother, against the Rothesay waves,
as though I wriggled to join some

frightening school. And when I went
to Torcello, to watch swifts twisting

into nests in the cathedral's eaves,
I passed that big green beetle,

rolling in a double tulip's blank
and crimson sunny heart. And when

I came back, hours after, and back;
walking one lane and waiting for

a boat, the bug was still there,
slowly turning around like a

half-woken dog. I thought of Corfu
Town, when we ate chicken in the square

and a wasp caught in your bikini top;
instantly the waiter was there

and with that courteous flick
that also cleared off crumbs, freed

both breast and insect into
the bright lunchtime air.

Pictish Whispers

What are the serrations down the tongue,
stitchings in the tissue of the language,
half-forgotten graftings of two strains
of rose, like a border between nations
that may tear
                    grandfather grammar from
the noise my mother tried to make
my playground larynx take
that now my lover hears as me?

There is a golf course, we laugh to learn,
that lies on the line between
being Danish or a Finn,
so that a ball, once driven, must cross
time's borders too,
and therefore spends an hour aloft
and lands a little altered, part-
meteor, part-albatross.

And sometimes on our alluvial lawn, on
the very green of our domesticity,
a little vowel will putt back to the past,
dislocating my identities like
the vertebrae of the neck,
suggesting that small congeries collect
like Pictish whispers, beneath
such incongruities as language can detect.

The act of translation is always with us,
touching us like love; why else
would the Italians crowd their ages
beneath the labial curtains
of a Madonna della Misericordia?
Why would they mingle with
their saints' Roman robes,
the modernity of armour on a frightened soldier?

Tintoretto paints his *Resurrection* in
sure knowledge that
such lightning can only strike us
now, cracking causality's mould:

all ages leap back from his Christ
as I did, at our kitchen sink,
when the thunderbolt seemed
to enter the room,
and suddenly, at my fingers' tips,
like a
      word unwantedly passing your lips,
I saw the spider.

First Gifts

(for David Clark)

Quartz, pebbled in the memory;
light in certain rooms partitioned

as it seems by stew-red curtains.
In one his bed, in the other a

piano I can't focus on through five-
year-old's eyes. A clockwork tank,

red and yellow studded metal,
small as a mechanical bird

I must have lost in one of those
tides, habits snarling like shingle

in the tug of years. Even the name
of his tenement's street, Cleghorn,

ceases to be our kind of sounds, and
moves, like insects in lichen, back

to its suggestive nest. Finally lost,
the one thing salvaged from his

vanishing, the pencil marks on blue
paper, thrown out by my mother,

one page of which showed him,
his face now seen as if through stone,

the other, through this fly's eye, this
pomegranate thought, cradling a nude.

The Cortina of the Isles

In the beginning was the Hillman, big green bulges
of indulgent metal, dark red leather, holding
my maternal ancestors, from which picnics were taken,
but which never really seemed to move.
Then came the Cortina, greener still, and
somehow sharper, a parter of
rain's shower-cloth, and the perspective's closing lanes,
departer to
                the ravelled roads of Ireland, where
my father drove into a great pig's behind,
printing our car's name
on innumerable slices of imaginary ham.

Now the journeys seem like nudges through
the reluctant curtains of the memory,
the air resisting like a hand,
smoothing the curls from my hair as we
near the sixties, knocking off
my father's glasses, and giving him those
of Roy Orbison, shoving between the clothes
hanging in my mother's wardrobe
for a raffia-like hat and larger buttons.

Now we depart for the islands as though
to visit the scattered images of relatives,
the lost interiors of houses in
Pembroke and Brechin.
I remember pointing to the gap between
my front teeth in a roadside snapshot;
the halo of rice around my first
beef curry, eaten in Oban; my father's rumour that
the currants could be swollen flies.

I remember all his driving
like Penelope listing
each of the patterns she picked out
each night, as the years passed: her
original design mutating
till it passed through as many stages as

the islands in
               her husband's wanders,
but each one blurred up with the next.

I remember this much of Skye: parking at
Dunvegan Castle, getting lost in white-
washed corridors, hung with tartan curtains.
We met an old woman who showed me
this fraying flag in a glass case:
she said the Fairies made it for
Clan MacLeod. Three times
its waving would ensure a victory,
and twice so far it had.
This was Dame Flora, apparently,
translucent as her never-to-be-brandished banner,
as though they were unweaving
together.

          By such means everywhere
that the Cortina went
became foreign, as
my father stitched them all to home.
By such driving he
concealed himself behind
the metal curtains
               of green car doors.

Mariposa Pibroch

If the Grunewald *Crucifixion*'s like
the skeleton of a butterfly, that

gnarling into the blackish, ragged
filaments through which my memory

is falling into the back garden
like pancake-large snowflakes;

then the mosquito I pressed against
this kitchen window yesterday,

the emptiness between its sap and
the pulse of my apologising finger,

is bringing me back, like swinging
from a balcony by the nail caught

in my jean's rump; landing in Elie,
in the grounds of a manse, cruciform,

clouting the earth like a sack
of floury potatoes, back emptied

of air. I'm facing a piper outside
Selfridges, playing airs sentimental

enough to summon drunks to shake
my penniless hands and beg; airs

that are built into the childhood
but aren't genuine. The giant

mosquito drone that alone demarks this
foreign music I feel kin to, salutes

or seems to the offerings I cannot
make: only the hearing is authentic.

II: SCHERZO

Dante Olive Oil

This exhaustive liquor of days,
of straining to see through it the ways

the heart's beast will not loup.
Fra Angelico would placate

this stumpish, coarse cat; a discourse
on the rich curtains of his nothingness

robes, his air. I am turned to an anterior
Italy, some infectious seed that,

bulging a vein, moled its way, in-
hering to the inner flaps like

the big dipper in Lido di Jesolo,
unsalted popcorn, a plastic cowboy

with basil neckerchief. It's like some
gimmick that grew, flip-flops or Flash

Gordon, that hideous stately daytrip,
waterbus across the glucose rhythms of

the lagoon, black streaks across
the Bridge of Sighs that were priests;

they seem Greek Orthodox or women.
Mother waits outside whilst we breathe

the sweltery melt of mosaics,
gold pooling in the beats of darkness.

Blue Shelter

Son et lumière at Miramare Castle on
the Venetian Riviera. I'm ten. A tape tells

the tragedy of Maximillian, first Emperor
of Mexico, and last. The voice-over is

by Andrew Cruickshank, 'a great Scottish actor',
recently dead. It takes me to a photo

from *Wonders of the World*, a book
of my grandfather's I can almost hear

in that voice. It takes me to Guanajuato,
where, in the rare aseptic crystal of the air,

bodies do not crumble. Propped like boards,
the mummies wait for God's last word

as flies wait for a spider. I pass
along this corridor of aunts and uncles.

At its end, before the last war began,
I see my grandmother board a tram

with half a pound of Braithewaite's tea.
Years later I will see a portrait on

a mummy-case in the British Museum:
Artemidorus. That was how my hair was cut

at ten. Memory's stained mirror sticks
at this face's background: time's blue shelter.

Composition with Seahorses

Out of the tangle at Trieste
of tramlines and memories, I scramble

like smoke from an oil: Giacomo
Joyce taught English there, moved

his mind a little out of the light
that, hitting Dublin's pavements at

its own angle, blinds the recorder's
eye. I learn perspective thus, looking

through train windows; cross the lagoon's
nuchal rail-line to Venice again.

The Grand Canal folds like a child's legs,
sat easy for the camera in the white

of my grandfather's arms, against
his garden fence. We buy two seahorses

where the motorboats land, dried
so that their tails form fragile

involutions. The map of this city has
fallen on my mind as softly as

a spider's web, catching on the face.
Its roads are made of stinking glass.

A woman chalks hopscotch on
the Campo for a child, then hops.

Cinema Paradiso

The visitor laughing in the kitchen now,
over the dash of her child from chair
to table, is much younger than
you realised she would be, pre-

viewing this scene twelve years ago,
leaning with your head full against
the narrow wooden funnel into
the Regal's balcony, a darning needle

holding the string of ticket halves,
holding a torch whose beam would only
touch the carpet. Up there was all
your eye could contact with, that screen

where you saw everything more
than once, where it permitted you
to gather up its instants. And now
your hearth is as far removed

from that other swing-like open stare,
Tay light through glass, wandered
eyebrows of the gulls, as it should be.
The woman painting soft seeds now,

in the room next door, is older, as
though fulfilling the former scale.
The telephone rings, you rise to talk
to a previous lover, childless.

Tiger Balm

The days are pressed like berries,
dried to sinew. Instead of this body
changing what I thought was me,
I've assumed the capability to change

through body everything that's thought.
I exercise my weaknesses into
a strained bridge bringing Cortinas
mainly, past crashes and crushings, the

old fear of having my patella
removed like a limpet by a bumper.
This comes back in cajuput, in paraffin:
I make a sweetmeat of my leg,

lavish it in liniment, *Tiger balm*,
and am returned to a two-roomed flat
in the Hilltown, Joe Flynn's,
who sat on people's joints and limbs

with hands like the Tay railbridge,
animate. I watch a thin fog of skin
gleam across the knowing tensions
of fingers delving after discs

and dislocating shoulders, re-
discovering the penitent frame in
a forced articulation, as though
he taught a language of bone.

This camphor-rich smearing in
my bedclothes brings him to me
as though my pains could shougle his
being into flesh again, but at

his facelessness the vision flies
like the tiger for a grey
balcony; out into a flag-day
of shirts, a circus of air

kept in the mind in which,
dangerously free, I see it burning
brighter than an injury, ready
to cauterise all memory.

The Land o' Cakes

(for Alec Esplin)

Perched in their multi-storey flat
like a well-fed eagle, the skin
around my small aunt's eyes splintered
with staring into needless distances.

As if her countryside was made of cakes
she swept up great trays for us,
while my uncle disgorged awful jokes
with Eric Morecambe-like insouciance.

A glass cabinet held miniature beers,
dustless undrunk guinnesses, light ales.
Once someone jumped from an upper floor
like jam on her spotless tablecloth.

She had diabetes suddenly; leaving
a ripped-off toe she plummetted too
in the hospital bed, grabbing onto us
like washing on the flashing balconies,

but she fell through pain like Alice
to me, and I thought she was constantly
halving her distance toward death
and would never smash, or like

an eagle losing its nerve, would pull
out of that dive. These days my uncle
stares at the distant bottles, stirs
his tea with a sugarless spoon.

Un Dizionario Immaginario

In the chill murmur of the rain
Venice exhales voices, like sighs

from ancient air, trapped
in bubbles in the ice cores

of the north. 'From the heath-
covered mountains of Scotia

I come,' pants a bottle of
unfamiliar whisky, faintly from

a window full of Dante olive oil.
We follow a trail of drips

across a bridge from a small berg
of mozzarella carried by

a cold-shouldered boy.
These signs concern us, mark

our passage as a breath on glass.
At night we follow our hotelier

past the shop of engravings:
the figure in its window whispers

'I am the man who lanterns lights.'
Last winter he fished the lagoon.

In the restaurant he led us to
the end of a soft roll

dipped in red wine
becomes the curl of a rose,

or a snail whose shell's colour
confuses the thrush.

The Surf Cookies

In the mornings we laugh in the red
café, make up songs for armadillos.

In the evenings we quarrel over cheap
Manhattans about a book we never write.

At night I rise to watch the lightning,
try to pull my thoughts out of our

connubial mesh; they don't come easily.
Legs are left sticking from previous

visits, previous visitors. Was it this
room we stayed in that night we found

the window had an outer curtain of
mosquitos, and a missing corner to

its pane? I remember Padua, which you
thought a bore, where I once heard

the extraordinary whine of pipers,
and a full band skirled round the hot

street's corner, playing what
should have been *Scotland the Twit.*

This tune is what we listen for
when we make up on waking, conglobe

ourselves again. Here the hearing is
already song; a finger's name appears

reversed, written on the glass:
we follow this signature's trail.

Parolla di Cavallo

Words like bees crawl over
my face and mouth: in the green

graveyard lizards fill the bay
leaves by Pound's grave with rustlings,

the voice of a British captain's stone:
'The heart knoweth its own

bitterness and the stranger
intermeddleth not therewith.'

Caught in the drain's grill after
the market's shut, white

cuttlefish beaks like eyeballs
blink, hard-lidded in the spray.

Sitting at the window in the
soft noise of night is piecing

entries together into
the sentences that accept,

watching our breathing as though
it held other entries,

eating *rocca* from a plastic bag,
rocket 'per il sogno'.

III: RONDO EL GRECO

I can't work out whether I'm mildly envious or faintly sceptical of
authors, poets, who can dredge up bucket after bucket of personal
sediment from way back, sift it, then hold up certain items said to
be of immense psychological importance.

SIMON ARMITAGE

Joe's Car
(for Joe Kelleher)

My first language was their bodies,
looking unconditionally up from a green

pram with wings like a Cortina.
Strange the phrases that come back in

the body's memory: a sensation of breasts
touching my upper arms' insides as I lie

on my side; a folding and a trampling
in, like Joe's car made of paint, that he

gave to me in a dream last night, messy
strips of white and red and blue I stamped

on into a more substantial version. My
grandmother found the Catholic green

unlucky, and my mother compensated with
a tacky rainbow, so we never knew

we shared a favourite. To prevent these
stutters between ages you must translate,

like Mirós into Hoppers, these brilliant
bubbles into loudnesses, burstings.

Return of the Tourist

There is a democracy among flies
I thought, staring at a swordfish

sprawled astonished on a plastic chair
in Roda Village. Eighteen years before

this, on the sand before this taverna
with its two olive trees in surf,

a great Greek mother smothered my mouth
with hot fatty lamb: in translation

a treat. Mother you said to spit it out
for the sandy-lipped alsatian:

no one saw me obey in that drunken
darkness, becoming separate for you.

Now Roda has exploded; our tacky shrapnel
has shattered its greying walls.

I fall back on a hill town with
one open restaurant, and no fish:

all it sells is lamb, that salacious memory.
As I eat a meatless omelette the family's

infant ambles over, mumbling through
a yellow pulp of chips he then spits

onto the laminated menu. Ingenuous,
this mess reminds me I can choose

among my links, my separations. I vote
to chew the lamb's fat. Delicious.

The Horse of the Years

Which particular is it that places
those grandparents' porch so nearly
always in sun, as if the cloud
alternatives were leaning away

from then? Is it harder to slot that
place into my darknesses, which
refuse to space regularly, filling
up this tilted end of the days.

I still think of them less often.
Paternal ancestors should
sweep over me like the shadows
of adults hurrying over children

down streets where darkness seems
locked into the tramlines. Not loss
then, but confusion at its lack,
like not finding their grave:

you walk up the rows like title-pages
of books you'll never read.
Inspect regiments busted to one rank.
All the names are as familiar as

the creed your ears had settled to
of birdsong in the silence on
the porch, knowing the exact height
of echoes over Kirkton, car-doors

closing. You realise as you don't
find their grave you think of it as
'hers'. What has been done with
his memories, these Catholics?

Backies, then, with your other grand-
father, who is also dead, but not
this far. You are looking down at
a hot stone in the grass, white

paint cruddled to it, stroked and
ribboned, baroque as the impact of
some dusty bird on glass. He tells
you how it came to be spilt.

The ghost of this bird batters at
the pane of dreams; perhaps it has
a message to pass between these
memories which cannot get through.

You are walking to the shed with
your grandfather. It has walking-sticks
with heads, each signed 'Kerkira' as
though this was his secret name.

I am climbing on that bright porch,
slipping between the poles that hold
it up like a spine-wide gate. I wait
my turn on the sheet-metal rocking horse

with my cousin on its painted back:
this is what will carry me away.

Panic in Dundee

'Thistles are easy,' the donkey remarked
to the olive tree it lived with in

the blue shade my mind had bottled
as soon as they were seen at Afionas;

'it's just that some of us are born
a stomach short of a good green meal.'

I watched them from behind fear's pane
as I circled the MacManus Galleries:

a glass beak pushed into that vein
down which the dumb thoughts speed,

the ones that can't conceive of accident.
The olive tree was pitted with Os,

as though the donkey still surprised it,
black hollows that ate heat. My attack

was clearing as I contemplated those
groves in which the green pips thicken

and nets held down by pebbles trawl
time for this sharp fruit. 'The thing

to grasp,' the donkey continued, 'is
not the thistle but the will that seeks

such indigestion; so vulnerable
a windfall will not be left unpecked.'

The broken bottle in the memory leaked:
these were the trees through which

the maddening god was glimpsed. Panic
of pigeons above Commercial Street.

I reached out my hand and found it able
to catch a blunted tumbling feather.

The Beano Elegies

(for Isabella Drew Powrie)

1

Every Saturday you brought us these
bright messages from the newsagent where
you worked after work, from cities
that were half Dundee, half desert;

somewhere that bears could live between
fairy tales, where children wore berets
like artists, top hats like no one else.
They were like us in that nothing changed:

the softy, once bashed, sprang up anew,
the greatest struggle was over being washed.
You reassured us, my cousin and myself,
with the smell of cheap paper, words

we could nearly read. You reassured us
with peppery soup, kail and lentils,
that nourishment could never end.
And yet leukaemia ate through you

into our safe lustrum; in all the photos
you are whiter than our smiles.
The ward was built on artificial slopes;
we rolled down them as you died.

2

The auld man couldn't hold us all –
never held him at all, my father said,
and so we loosened from the so-called
clan, lost all with my gran, his mother.

The auld man had been quite a dandy;
rolled his own from a silvery case,
kept his sleeves up with gleaming bands,
played the murderer once in *Arsenic*

and Old Lace. That was the kind of
face he still possessed, an easy man
to hate. His other children gave
birth to other cousins in my place.

The auld man played the clarinet
in the thirties, busked 'for the rent';
his wife raised five in Ann Street's fug,
he slept in the hedges like a speug.

The auld man was white trash, then,
who worked his wife into her grave,
he thought a bought house was a waste
of cash; he never, ever saved.

3

Billy the Cat no longer leaps
on criminals like a British panther.
Um tribe of Little Plum has been
wiped out by some cartoon germ.

Biffo lost his cover and his tongue
and cannot now complain his friends
and he are no longer drawn
by their originating artists.

Every Saturday these comics come;
mutations, like the memories they cause,
yet living. The Catholic who lacked
love, and so became devoid of grace.

The martyr to motherhood who proved
all mothers therefore must be good.
Behind the comics stood that couthy
ruthlessness the press baron, unionless.

Behind these paper ancestors stands
the protestant in me, issueless:
her eyes, bruised blue with illness,
his throat where the cancer got hold.

Other Tongues

I picked up a pebble on the olive-
brown path round the back of
Afionas on the island of Corfu,
cream-coloured like an old knee-cap.

It sat in the hook of my fingers
with a hollow for my thumb
as though it asked to be thrown
out over the slopes blurred purple

with wild thyme, back to the crowd
that clattered in the swell. It said
other tongues have spat me out
but none so eloquent as water.

I took it back to my hotel. It said
other tongues gall you because
you've spent so much time
shuffling the beach of your own.

Other tongues lick at your ear
in the big night of your ignorance
while the sticks of your own country,
that was once one forest, drift

back slowly, to smoke in the grate
of your belly, and never catch.
Other tongues try to shove their fierce
red meat of difference down your

throat, while your tongue wallows
in the blue shell of a shut palate.
That's all your grip can know,
the pebble said, so let me go.

I said I will learn rhetoric from
this stone, and took it home.
I have another tongue in my head
the like of which it's never heard.

Dingle Dell

There is no passport to this country,
it exists as a quality of the language.

It has no landscape you can visit;
when I try to listen to its vistas

I don't think of that round tower, though
only two exist in Scotland, though

both are near me. There are figures on
an aunt's old clock, cottars; Scots

as marketed to Scots in the last century:
these are too late. I seek something

between troughs, a green word dancing
like weed in a wave's translucence,

a pane not smashed for an instance
through which the Dingle Dell of Brechin

sinks into the park like a giant's grave
from which his bones have long since

walked on air. Into this hole in
the gums of the language I see a name

roll like a corpse into the plague pits:
Bella. It is both my grandmothers'.

Beauty, resilient as girstle, reveals
itself: I see all of Scotland

rolling down and up on death's yoyo.
There is no passport to this country.

THE LANDFISH:

AND OTHER POEMS

Ode to the Dictionary

(translated from the Spanish of Pablo Neruda)

Spine o an aiver, a stirk
fit fur thi darg, seestimatic
fat almanac:
as a cheild
Eh cut yi deid, thocht
Eh kent ut aa,
that aa ma leir
wiz bettir than yir leid,
an lyk a po-fissd puddock
Eh wad puff 'Eh get
ma vocab
straicht an steaman fae
Moont Sinai.
Eh sall translate
aa foarms tae alchemy.
Eh am thi dominie.'

Thi heid dominie kept mum.

Thi Dictionair
auld-spauldit in uts shauchilt
leathir jaiket
sat quietlike,
uts puissance dernit.

But wan dey,
eftir Eh'd trehd ut
and decrehd ut,
crehin ut as
yissless assa cuddie oanna motirwey,
when fur months syne, withoot a mump,
ut hud din as ma deas
an thi heff o ma heid,

aiver: workhorse; *stirk:* young bullock; *darg:* day's labour; *cheild:* young man; *leir:* learning; *leid:* language; *po-fissd:* stuck-up; *puddock:* toad; *puff:* boast; *fae:* from; *dominie:* master, teacher; *kept mum:* said nothing; *spauldit:* shouldered; *shauchilt:* worn, misshapen; *dernit:* hidden; *cuddie:* horse; *mump:* complaint; *deas:* seat; *heff o ma heid:* favoured spot of my head (pillow).

ut loupt-thi-tethir an plantit
uts heels oan ma hallan-stane,
an spangit up, shaukin uts laives
an thi nests o uts nieves,
spreidan thi crop o uts fullyery,
ut wiz
a tree,
a nachural,
fouthy
aipple-glory, aipple orchart, aipple tree,
an wurds
skinkilt innuts coontliss brainchis,
pearly or murmellan,
a goshens o speak i thi blauds,
chairgit wi truth an soond.

Eh
pairt
twa o uts
pages:
Cappilow
Capshon
whit a giftie tae
pree these keesty
syllabuls,
an, furthir doon,
Carcant,
jist waitin oan a lassie's craig,
and ithirs,
Car-cleuch, Carcuddoch, Cardecue,
Cardower an *Cardin,*
parlins
as souple as thi fleesh o plooms,
pattir pappin i thi licht
lyk deltit seeds that delve

---

loupt-thi-tethir: rebelled; *hallan stane:* doorstep; *spangit:* leapt; *nieves:* fists; *crop:*
highest growth; *fullyery:* foliage; *aipple-glory:* blossom; *skinkilt:* sparkled, shone;
murmellan: sonorous; *goshens:* great abundance; *blauds:* leaves; *cappilow:* out-
distance, to outdo another in reaping; *capshon:* windfall; *giftie:* rare skill; *pree:*
taste; *keesty:* flavoursome; *carcant:* a garland of flowers for the neck; *craig:* throat;
car-cleugh: left hand; *carcuddoch:* intimate; *cardecue:* silver coin; *cardower:* mender
of old clothes; *cardin:* a rare trout found in Loch Leven; *parlins:* expressions; *souple:*
soft; *plooms:* plums; *pappin:* bursting; *deltit:* withdrawn.

i thi dreels o vocabulair
veive again an geean life:
yince mair thi hert is kempin them.

Dictionair, you arena a
cairnie, a deid-hoose, a graff,
a burian, a howff,
but shenachie,
shielit bleeze,
rigg o berialls,
ayebidand,
granitar o dialecks.
It is a ferly tae
recognosce in your collations
leid
o thi forerinners,
thi austrous and
lang-forleitit
saw, a
son o Scota,
dreean lyk
an eldren pleuch,
as boondit in uts yiss
as an auldfarrant graith,
kept
i thi perjink peen that cut
a cheengeliss Pictish profile.
Or anithir
wurd
that we find tint
atween thi nucks
that brently seems

dreels: rows; *veive:* beautiful, lively; *kempin:* harvesting; cairnie: memorial heap of stones; *deid-hoose:* sepulchre; *graff:* grave; *burian:* tumulus; *howff:* cemetery; *shenachie:* bard, teller of old stories; *shielit:* protected; *bleeze:* blaze; *rigg:* field; *berialls:* precious stones, fine crystals; *ayebidand:* eternal; *granitar:* official in charge of a granary; *ferly:* marvel; *recognosce:* to resume possession of, identify, acknowledge, revise; *collations:* pooling of inheritances with a view to their equitable distribution amongst the heirs; *austrous:* severe; *forleitit:* abandoned; *dreean:* enduring; *eldren:* ancient; *pleuch:* ploughshare; *boondit in uts yiss:* bounded in its use; *auldfarrant:* old-fashioned; *graith:* tool; *perjink:* exact; *peen:* hammerstroke of a mason; *tint:* lost; *nucks:* lines; *brently:* suddenly.

as sair-fu an lithe i thi mou
as a hazelnut
or juicy as a plundirt pear.

Dictionair, lat wan
pinkie frae yir thoosan hauns, wan
bort frae yir thoosan emerants,
wan
single
drap
fae yir maiden waatirs, lat
wan dram
frae
yir distellit fallachan
faa
jist
when Eh need ut
oan ma lips
an thi tip o ma biro,
intae ma olivetti.
Frae thi dens an thi hauchs
o yir dinnelin wuid
gee me,
whan Eh waant ut thi maist
wan jenny-wren, brustin wi sang,
thi seil o a single droney-bee,
wan splinnir fae
yir birkenshaw o Caledon, scentit wi
millennia o pine,
wan
syllabul,
wan thrum, wan soond,
wan seed:
fur Eh am yirdy an wi wurds Eh sing.

sair-fu: tasty; *lithe:* smooth; *mou:* mouth; *plundirt:* stolen by children; *emerants:*
emeralds; *dram:* measure of whisky; *distellit:* distilled; *fallachin:* concealed store;
hauchs: land by rivers; *dinnelin:* reverberating; *seil:* gift; *droney-bee:* bumble-bee;
splinner: splinter; *birkenshaw:* forest; *thrum:* tremor; *yirdy:* earthy.

Location Shot

I thi Carse
i thi hill's lee
a clearin inna copse
beatan wi
thi guns ahent
Eh see a deer
a human length awa
an faa
thi heid explodin
green aa owre me, aa
faain and explodin
pale green as
leaves' ablows
an follyan those
thi deavenin
shout o thi shot
thi snot gun
meanin
thi deer an me
wan corse
hit thi Carse
haurd
an find ut saft.

Carse: the Carse of Gowrie, the river plain north of the Tay between Dundee and Perth; *ahent:* behind; *ablows:* undersides.

Ode to Tesco's

(for James Meek)

Hail to thee TESCO'S oan thi Esplanade,
thi grechtest ferly that Dundee huz made,
better by far than thi auld Tay Brig,
given that a bauld man disna need a stick, he needs a wig.

Twas in thi year o 1990,
which Eh'll remembir as lang as Eh've a mind tae,
that TESCO'S came oor way,
resolved fur a few years tae profitably prey
upon thi siller o thi fowk o Tay.

Amang thae brichtsome dreels,
verdant as thi Carse's leas,
weavirs' weans may browze fur farls,
and also fur frozen peas.
Roond teabags, polystyrene stovies,
and cans o Grannie's soup:
that's thi stuff tae pick yi up,
should yir speerits droop.
Aa thi fruits o progress ur
available oan shelves,
plus some fruits frae Sooth Afrika,
that land o happy elves.

Ut used tae be thi Empire
that brocht us wir bananas,
but noo, thanks tae grecht TESCO'S,
we've jam fur wir todays
an jam fur wir mañanas.
And nivir mind thi marmalade
that used tae be made here:
ut still sez 'Dundee' oan ut,
sae ut huz tae be guid gear.

In fact that is anither thing
tae TESCO'S that we aawe:
gif ut wisnae fur thi labellin,
we widnae ken fuck aa.
Gif ut wisnae fur thi labellin
tae keep thi puntirs right,

hoo'd we be able tae tell
which puddin wiz black and which wuz white?
Gif ut wisnae fur thi labellin
tae keep us puntirs right,
hoo wid we tell a sassidge roll
frae yir aiverage pile o shite?
Gif Dundee wisnae labelt
thi city o 'Discoveree',
hoo'd we be able tae tell ut frae
yir run o thi rin-doon auld mill touns
dumpit by thi sea?

Epilogue

Twas in thi year o 1991,
a palindromic sonovabitch gif ivir Eh saw wan,
that Eh feenisht this, meh latest ode,
which thi fowk o Dundee wull nivir see, by Gode,
unless Eh pent ut oan thi auld Perth Road.
In which case, gif Eh'm no arrestit,
therr's a couple o dugs it micht keep interestit,
and, gif Eh am, some late nicht TESCO shoppirs
may pondir wha's thon gettin beat up by thi coppirs?
afore they daundir hame
mebbe tae luke up meh name
in Billy Kay's *Buik o Dundee*
tho, bein frae Ayrshire, he's nivir heard o me,
nor, bar wan reference, o michty MAGONNAGAL,
which maun that rare speerit sairly appal,
but thigithir we'll huddle
in the bandstand o thi Magdalen Green;
Eh'll cuddle a boattul, he'll cuddle thi auld Queen,
and thigithir praise TESCO'S, maist magnificent tae be seen,
better by faur than thi auld Blackness Skail, than Haakhill
        or thi Overgate, than Genril Monk's Hoose or thi Royal
        Airch, or thi Pillars or thi Wellgate,
gif yi ken whit Eh mean.

ferly: marvel; *dreels:* rows; *aawe:* owe; *daundir:* stroll.

NOTE: All the buildings listed at the end of this poem have been demolished.

Bluebottle Bella

(for Isobel Neil)

Thi ainguls waulk upon
Heaven's flair wi sookie-feet,
wi galaxies fur een
as oan thi Earth they leet.

Thi gress hiz jist been mown
an Granda muves atween
thi roseis an thi palm trees,
tweelin grey thru green.

Thi bakiry gees aff a gust
o breid lyk a spang-new cod
an aa thi ainguls trummil,
caucht i thi wab o Gode.

Thi gless ut treetuls doon thi fremm
thi gulls slip owre thi rivir,
thi rowld-up Tully ut descends
an blauds thum oot furivir.

een: eyes; *leet:* inform, comment; *tweelin:* weaving; *gust:* taste, smell; *spang-new:* brand new; *cod:* pillow; *treetuls:* trickles; *Tully:* 'Evening Telegraph', a Dundee paper; *blauds:* batters, pokes with the end of something.

Bannockburn the Movie

Inna fillum in ma heid
wi Errol Flynn an Gary Coopir
thi Black Douglis flings a hert
ahead o hum intae
a Saracenic fuge
in jist thi wey that Eh fling mine
intil oor swack o days.

In jist thi wey thi ainguls lab
planits inna kype o stars.
And in thi movie Robert Wagner as
de Brus is waatchin thon
waabilt wabstir slair
threids lyk smirr aa owre
thi windie o'iz modish antir.

Ut gets monochrome.
Wur goamin thru thi gloamin
camera, an aathin's Italianate:
smokin in thi blue licht maks
him lyk a star frae
an auldir systum
in sum wey that meisures wi

thi joco twist we did afore
oor Gaggia thon Christmas.
Geoarge Sandirs oanna Vespa wull
ride up tae challenge Bruce,
an you wull caa me
tae cappucino. Thi fillum wull
pley oot tae a toom theatur.

Thi stars keep birlan in
wir wamplin heids. We dwell
in deys as dae thi ainguls
in Paradise, stowffin oan
thir glessy pletties,
braithin freedom anerly
thru thir heels.

Un Memoriam

Thi tide ligs twa tawny lines
o reeds an black sea weeds
and oak leaves roond ma feet

lyk bitten-thru haufs o a wreath.
Thi tide rowls a boattul oan
thi stanes wi a saft clinclank.

Blue braks thru thi fungal layirs
o clood, while a cormorant
freaks oot thi wee shrill gulls

that rant awa fur lampies
while ut vanishes within thi Tay's
lang mercury mooth

lyk an iley toothpick.
Thi cauld seeps oot thi guschets
o'ur humirless smile.

Thi pennt that Eh wance scellit
here hiz jist aboot flakit awa;
a straucht streak o white

hauf clings hauf peels lyk lichen
or lyk a dreebul doon Tay's stane lip
fae sum mythic lithic fellatio.

Thi licht furs thru thi cloods
an spools upo thi waatir.
Gif Tay wiz film ut wad

hae nithin tae show but air
fur aa uts years, sma snottirs
o a plane gaun owre

Bannockburn the Movie: *intil:* into; *swack:* splash, swallow of drink; *lab:* throw; *kype:* ring for playing marbles; *waabilt:* unsteadied; *wabstir:* spider; *slair:* smear; *antir:* cave; *goamin:* to gaze about wildly or idly; *toom:* empty; *birlan:* spinning; *wamplin:* gently flowing; *stouffin:* stomp or plod along; *pletties:* balconied tenements.

Un Memoriam: *ligs:* lies; *lampies:* lampposts; *guschets:* corners; *scellit:* spilled; *fae:* from; *snottirs:* snot running from a child's nose.

lyk this spill o pennt,
thi saft antrin blotchis o
big boats' bahookies lyk

thi bruises oan a pear. Ut isna
that we micht as well
no be therr, ut's that we canna,

save by pollution's langir-lastin
ejaculaishun, be mair.

A Dream of the River

Ma bauky burd that sooms ablow thi waves,
man's albatross that dines oan abalone
an dees in thoosans i thi nylon nets
aff frae Japan: Hell's chorus, corybants
whas cymbals ur propellors girdin i thi lift
till licht's haurd loof maks granks o
aa that sang, slappin oan yir droonit heid:
whit noyades hae yi no seen, yi naiads o
Ocean's dwaumy linns, whit kinks an
loundirs i thi shallows, whit a slatch o sleein
fae yir brither wi thi slammach in his heid,
auld able-boukit Cain hissel?

An yet he cams tae peer, tae pree this element
lyk syrup inniz thocht, sklaichan'iz tung aroond
thi mappamundi's quaich, laivan a kneggum o'um
aa airts that winna waash awa,
pleyin Mozart tae thae waarm fishes
afore he feeds thum till'iz pets,
thi scurry whelps an baudrins that'll pit
a paaprint til'iz celsitude.
Hoo few hae jist kickt aff fae seean's hull,
nae kippage o connectin's lorn, nae rumpshun o
be this be thon, nin o rummle-gumpshun's spawn
at aa, nae fear o scowdies or
o runkirs' jaas, thi slyrey feel o scrow's feet,
a rothick rinnin thru the lang
sheemach o thi sea
fae Aberbrotherick tae Crail:

bauky burd: bat; *sooms:* swims; *ablow:* below; *girdin:* performing vigorously; *loof:* palm of the hand; *granks:* groans; *dwaumy:* dreamy; *linns:* currents; *kinks:* spasmodic chokings; *loundirs:* the dealing out of heavy blows; *slatch:* messy work; *slammach:* cobwebs; *able-boukit:* able-bodied; *pree:* taste; *sklaichan:* beslobbering; *quaich:* drinking-cup; *kneggum:* disagreeable taste; *scurry:* despicable; *baudrins:* cats; *celsitude:* highness; *kippage:* confusion; *rumpshun:* uproar; *rummlegumpshun:* common-sense; *scowdies:* jellyfish; *runkirs:* lumpfish; *jaas:* jaws; *slyrey:* fine, like linen; *scrow:* shrimp; *rothick:* young edible crab; *sheemach:* tangle or matted mass of hair etc.

Eh sloomd thi ithir nicht a tree
wiz traddelin thi Tay, sae aa uts brainches
besommed i thi waatirs, rode thir roils an routies
lyk bowdirs i thi wuids. Whaur uts ruits cuid be
Eh cudna tell, but aa uts laives werr braggir-coorse,
thir keest wiz slattyvarryish, sae sharrow oan
thi tung. Eh wiz waulkin thi logs as tho Eh werr
a wee weavir pent in Brobdignag,
warkin oot a purfloe oan an ettin's loom,
MaGonnagal wi wurds tae threid,
Penelope whas tapestry aye hung in tantirwallops,
a tickler furra man tae read.

Eh wiz singan grey thrums til a wumman
i thi sweel an swatch o waatir till
Eh saw thi mere-swine risin lyk rubigos in droves,
scores o Ratatosks aa fu o thi warld's clash,
rovin i thi dreels o roukit green,
thi draiggilt rabble o thi laives
that moupt thi fish an mizzelt awa, geean noo
hauf a squirl then mollopin, stottin noo
an stendin next, until ut seemd a speak wiz
aa aroond me, i thi braal o soonds an muveins
spirlan aa aboot. But whit that sang wiz
wha can tell that wears thi mow-band wurds
gin Eh sang ti men aa Eh heard then
ut wad hae aa thi rhetory o rewellan burds:
Eh cudna keep ma hungir oot fur mair.

Frae sicca vaige yi dinna quite revert,
feart as wun is tae dream sae deep, tae be
thi steethe-stane let doon i thi harns.
Eh'm still waulkin oan thi stell waatirs
that wear thi starns an Tayport's lampies
i thir herr an lat thum share thi gree,
Eh still allow that matter huz uts ginks,
uts gillatrypes in whilk yi are thi coryphee,
thi wan wha mudgis whit oor symbuls canna say.

54

Sythe

Thi swift
    that draps
frae thi nest intae flicht
wull fleh owre thi taps
o thi dey an thi nicht
fehv thoosan mile
wull hear uts skryle
while three year
wull pass inna breer
nor wull ut rest
till ut biggs uts ain nest
this Eh attest:

Guidbye.
    Livan oan
thi ootside o thi sky
or wi you by
isnae much o a choice
gin yi waant ma voice
no tae mell wi yir ain
lyk saalt waatir wi rain
gin yi waant me tae heal
skaiths Eh can't feel
gin yi waant me tae grow
or jist go:

A Dream of the River: *sloomd:* dreamt; *traddelin:* trampling; *besommed:* broomed, swept; *roils an routies:* angry little motions; *bowdirs:* squalls; *braggir-coorse:* like a coarse seaweed; *keest:* taste; *slattyvarryish:* like edible seaweed; *sharrow:* bitter; *purfloe:* edging; *ettin:* giant; *tantirwallops:* tatters; *singan grey thrums:* purring; *sweel an swatch:* the swirling pattern; mere-swine: dolphins; *rubigos:* penises; *Ratatosk:* the squirrel who climbs the world-tree in Norse mythology; *clash:* gossip; *dreels:* rows as in a berry field; *roukit:* misty; *draiggilt:* wet; *moupt:* nibbled; *mizzelt:* melted, vanished; *squirl:* flourish; *mollopin:* tossing the head disdainfully; *stottin:* moving erratically; *stendin:* moving purposefully; *braal:* fragmented mass; *spirlan:* whirling; *mow-band:* halter; *rhetory:* eloquence; *rewellan:* bamboozling; *vaige:* voyage; *steethe-stane:* the first of the stones let down as an anchor to deep-sea fishing-lines; *stell:* steep; *gree:* honour; *ginks:* tricks; *gillatrypes:* witches' dances; *mudgis:* hints at.

Sythe: *sythe:* satisfaction, compensation; *skryle:* shriek; *breer:* sprint; *biggs:* builds; *skaiths:* hurts.

Snow
>wull bandage thi groond
whaur therr's nae wound
thi buried wurd
wull live withoot soond
withooten wan burd
thi sky is attuned.
Whaur Eh land
nithin is planned
wha Eh mate
is separate.

Winter Prayer

Gowd maun gleet ablow thi groond
inna lang saft blintir as
a waatirgaw waulks ower Fife,
follyin thi train Eh'm lukein frae.

Ma haunds muve thigithir smooth
as saut waatir mellin wi fresh:
Lord, therr issa spidir
drinkin at meh hert's quaich.

She has a pearl o meh aynd
caucht i thi starnie o'ur lends,
waash hir awa wi a pirl
fae yir fingir's prisum.

Fill ma lungs wi toyts o braith
ma hert wi rubyellie bluid
and oan ma tung pit gowd,
since Eh maun sing.

gleet: glitter; *ablow:* below; *blintir:* gleam; *waatirgaw:* indistinct rainbow; *quaich:* drinking cup; *aynd:* breath; *starnie:* star; *lends:* loins; *pirl:* touch; *toyts:* freshwater pearls found in the Tay; *rubyellie:* liquor made of rubies.

Sny

(in Beckley)

I thi oor afore thi voices cum
lyk midgis tae this plum

pub gairden whaur
evenin leans upo thi bar,

trees' anguls hintin at
thi tilt o licht's hat,

we sit and read o thi amorous mime
twa slugs perform wi a baa o thir slime

and an unnamed burd o prey
laives uts creh inna fruit-tree's splay.

An then thi weel-heelt puntirs came:
Eh caucht masel bleezin, assignin blame

no tae thir accents but
til these stevins' vacant note,

an kent ut still a dispersonin scheme
tae faa back here oanna Scoattish dreme.

Thir bairns rise lyk eisenin gulls
til th'intirmittent pulse

o ripe plums faain, thon dirdin clyte
o purpie fruct aa reekt in white

that waukens us fae time
as tho thi stars geed a bluey skime

afore they sklytit doon,
an space's outh wiz beamfu wi this tune

that pangs a keelie's thrappil
an fills thi wurm that pangs thi appil

an fills yir een wi gloamin
as licht gaes thru thi fruit-trees' strummin.

A Three Year Ode

I *To Gorbachev* (1991)

> *For now in the flower and iron of the truth*
> *To you we turn...*
> HUGH MacDIARMID
> First Hymn to Lenin

Thi cat sits at ma French windies,
irrepressibil, stupit, lyk thi licht
that maun cam in, she moans.

Ut's a cauld dey, thi waurmth oan ma herr,
lyk hir affeckshun, anerly exists
atween thi gless an me. Ootwith

ut aa blaws loose as meh attenshun
when Eh lat hur in. She waants
aa o me or oot again. Eh sit an feel

licht fill thi hooses in Fife
an the cheek banes o Tay's waves,
Eh rowl wi ut lyk thi cat owre

thi Baltic. Eh'm oan a trenn o licht
speedin fur Moscow, bearin Pasternak
back, shovelt oot o Zhivago's snaa-cell.

Eh'm oan a trenn o licht speedin
atween thi gless an thi sel,
enterin Russia oan a cat's shouthirs.

Eh'm fu o thi eisenin that wad stoap time
i thi middil o thi page, an force
uts maist donsy passengir

oot, tae dance upo thi snaw. Dance,
Liberty, dance! spleet yir sark an
melt aa permafrost wi yir reid wame!

Sny: *Sny:* effect of light through branches; *bleezin:* furious; *stevins:* voices; *dispersonin:* treating with indignity; *eisenin:* desirous; *dirdin:* resounding; *clyte:* rap; *purpie:* purple; *fruct:* fruit; *reekt:* smoked; *skime:* gleam; *sklytit:* fell heavily; *outh:* outermost parts; *beamfu:* full to the rafters; *pangs:* packs; *keelie:* hawk.

A Three Year Ode: *maun:* must; *anerly:* only; *eisenin:* desire; *donsy:* lovely, vigorous; *sark:* undergarment; *wame:* belly or womb.

But Liberty nivir fed onywan. An Christ's
poke, tho unca deep, wisna designd
tae clear thi queues, 'Thi puir ur aye wi us.'

Thi licht mairches thru Leningrad streets
back frae Afghanistan, fae Germany.
Thi licht wad faa oan onywan.

Ut pleys wi ma herr, burns ma nape,
ut passis thru ma banes an laives spores
therr o daurkniss ayont aa dawins.

Thi cat dwaums o parlaments
o heidliss mice. Eh'm lukein thru'ur
intil thon nicht ayont bombs, ayont money,

whaur fowk stoap oan brigs owre thi Clyde,
thi Neva, an waatch thi licht arrive
fae extink stars, an wait fur thi licht

fae thi stars yet tae come.

II *To Yeltsin* (1992)

> *I am dead, but you are living*
> BORIS PASTERNAK
> Doctor Zhivago

As thi furst bids arrehv fur Lenin's banes
twa blimps ascend abune Red Square:
yin says *Pola*, thi ithir *Cola*. Ilkane

costs saxty thoosan dollars. Thi date
is May thi Furst, but nae tanks gee thanks
tae you, as ye maun've calculatit

lang syne. Thi furst buds push thru
this English gairdin lyk fingirtips:
Eh wundir gin Eh tuke thir prints

wad Eh get sodgers, husbands, Man-
delstam? An yet ye hud tae repress
thon camsteery core o celebrants

poke: pouch; *unca:* very, unusually, awfully; *ayont:* beyond; *dawin:* dawn; *dwaums:*
dreams; *abune:* above; *camsteery:* fierce, perverse; *core:* group.

o Stalin's burthday – sae Freudian
an act ut wad be tactless tae add
thi Capitalist's platitude

concernin thi Unearnin's gratitude
gin ye didnae sae brawly deserve ut
fur duntin yir last heid-bummir oot,

wha wadna hasten Russia's race
tae buy hur freedom frae thi West
when serfitude wiz aa yi could

invest. Eh waatch thi dentylions
brent thru thi southren simmer green
lyk black mairt brollies, bairgain boambs,

or jist thi plooks oan thi Urse's hide
as seen frae space by Krikalev,
thon cosmonaut that sat ootside

aa cheenge, angelickly-aware
thru radio hams o coup an you,
o Commonwealth an thon's despair,

thi last tae ride thi yirthly crest,
thi furst tae cross owre concepts; no
thi achronic birl o dogma's collar.

Eh think o Scoatlan, still stapt ticht
in uts disunity, lyk Auld Nick's
three-heidit doag in wan slip leash;

and Dante wiz sae subtly richt
tae tell himsel tae nivir retour,
no jist tae Florence, his past hame,

but tae thi past in Florentine heids,
thir indecisive noo. Dundee
wad be lyk landin fae thon heicht,

breathan thi Steppes' uncheengin air.

---

heid-bummir: leader; *dentylions:* dandelions; *brent:* burst or leap; *black mairt:*
black market; *urse:* bear; *stapt:* rammed; *retour:* return.

III *To Rutskoi* (1993)

Our concern is human wholeness – the child-like spirit
Newborn every day –
HUGH MacDIARMID
Third Hymn to Lenin

As Eh exhaled, trehin tae relax,
Eh heard thi saulter i thi field ootside
whinny, and Eh thocht o thon

puir cuddie in Kutznetsky Street
that Mayakovsky waatcht faa doon,
be whuppit as ut pechd uts life awa.

That wiz whit yi ettlet tae dae
tae thon sair forfochen nag
caad 'Communism' thi ither dey.

Did you no ken tho histry micht
repeat, lyk a wean that huztae eat
naethin but the rehet kail o

slaistery theory, ut nivir can
repeal utsel? Eh luke oot meh windie at
thae horsis that, like me, nivir hud

tae pu as muckle's Orwell's Boxer,
an think we hae medd fictions here
o yir followers' rarest hopes;

fur whit wiz Timex but a tale telt
tae richtless warkirs by thir
virrless union, tae keep thum aa

fae kennan o thir knackirt faa
intae fause timelessness, thi pasture
o a militatin posture.

Aa you did wiz add some killin,
tae mak ut mair Leniny, tae gee ye mair
1917-esque a feelin.

trehin: trying; *saulter:* a horse that jumps in events; *cuddie:* a horse; *pechd:* panted; *ettlet:* attempted; *sair forfochen:* very bewildered, exhausted; *rehet:* reheated; *slaistery:* slimy, unpalatable; *as muckle's:* as much as; *virrless:* impotent; *fause:* false.

61

An sae thi tincan cavalry came at last
but no tae sain ye by thi pooer
o thi haimmer an Rab Sorbie,

but, fur twa an a plack o promises
fae Yeltsin, tae mak thi nicht
a dingle-dousie o tracer fire,

a swack an dinnil o rinny daith
in oaffices and oan stairwells. Still
Eh'm vanein at thon gripy bairn,

ridan oan thi back o a bear,
bringan thi Apocalypse o statelessness,
thi furst lowsan-time

o thi reins an bridle o thi harns.

---

sain: protect from harm by a ritual sign; *Rab Sorbie:* sickle; *twa and a plack:* a
considerable amount; *dingle-dousie:* a lighted stick waved rapidly in the dark to
form an arc of light; *swack:* a sudden heavy blow; *dinnil:* vibration; *vanein:* calling
a horse in harness to turn to the left; *lowsan-time:* the time for unyoking horses
and stopping farmwork; *harns:* brains.

Selkie Sang

Eh waulk a lingle-back o links
an loans asleep but feelan wi ma feet
fur uts rigg-banes o sailors' graves
that wad nivir be by
grecht Tay o thi waves.

Innuts lippirs an the swires Eh meet
yir een's schine sae innerly
sae sune, ut seems a ferly
fae twa seals' heids,
thir nid-nidy-noy that sinks
an sloitirs neat
's a tung atween twa leids.

Awaash wi mair o memries than
ur livan, this waatir rinks
us, nae limits tae uts scoupin ban.

---

selkie: seal (believed by the Gaelic peoples to be be capable of human form); *lingle-back:* a long weak back; *links:* sea-meadows; *rigg-banes:* vertebrae; *lippir:* a slight swell or ruffle on the surface of the sea; *swire:* a declivity; *ferly:* marvel; *fae:* from; *nid-nidy-noy:* bobbing motion, as though one were going to sleep; *sloitir:* to engage in wet work; *leid:* language; *rinks:* surrounds; *scoupin:* dancing; *ban:* ring.

Slowdive

Hoo slaw this humplin
spinnir o wir banes
aboot thi luvin-bed:

oor fleesh is pirlin awa
behind'um lyk twa
maas oanna updraucht,

this pirrie o breath
wi baith hae draan,
this wan insook.

Yi splash yir herr aboot
thi sheets, Eh shew
a sark o men an weemen

tae hap aboot a wan,
thi wean unsoucht as yet
but waitin oan

yir wame's ingyne.
This island o lorn flochts
whaur we meet

as gendirs, cloven
or foarkit, whaur we dehv
as slaw's twa whales,

unpursuivet.

Hoo slaw: how slow; *umplin:* humping the shoulders; *spinnir:* a spiral movement; *pirlin:* twisting; *maas:* seagulls; *updraucht:* updraught; *pirrie:* a tiny breeze; *insook:* an inrush; *shew:* sew; *sark:* shirt; *wame's:* womb's; *ingyne:* genius, ingenuity; *lorn:* desire.

Three Sonnets by Raphael

1

Ma luve, yi mesmerd me wi twa braw lichts,
thae bluachie een that mak me maundir, thrieve-
less, oan yir cheeks as snaa-beds, lips rose-vieve:
yir ain clear clash mair fairly frames sic sichts.

Eh bleeze sae bremeish Tay hirsel, wi a sea
thrown in, 's a dreme o steam. Eh am glad wuid,
that skin an birn diz burn tae this wan guid:
sic blethirs gee ma wull tae walloch swee.

Sae donsy is thi draucht an crookit threid
o airms an crammas herr across ma craig
that lowsan-time wad mak a wickit meid.

O mony sonsy sma things Eh stey vague;
by sic screeds mair nor lugs ur rendirt deid,
sae Eh bide mum o whaur ma thochts stravaig.

2

As Jesus wiz a blindan gleesh tae Paul,
thrawn awald, wurdliss fur whit he discernit;
jist sae meh hert is happed, ma thochts ur dernit:
luv's reek lyk Isis casts a vellous caul.

Tharefore thi muckle that Eh saw and did
is aa translatit intae gaudy leid,
hert's tickety stangs – till grey hiz tappd ma heid
Eh'll no let oan (lyk Paul, Eh'm unca-guid).

1: *bluachie:* pale blue; *maundir:* babble; *thrieveless:* thriftless; *vieve:* vivid; *clash:* conversation; *bleeze sae bremeish:* burn so fiercely; *skin an birn:* entirely; *blethirs:* nonsense, also bellows; *walloch:* dance, romp; *donsy:* neat, suitable; *draucht:* (cart) load; *crammas:* crimson; *craig:* throat; *lowsan-time:* when the yoke is taken off a work animal; *meid:* fate; *sonsy:* lovely; *screeds:* lists; *mum:* silent; *stravaig:* wander.

2: *gleesh:* flame; *thrawn awald:* tossed onto one's back like a drunkard; *dernit:* hid; *reek:* smoke; *vellous:* velvety; *leid:* language; *stangs:* thrills; *unca-guid:* over-virtuous.

Meh sowel's as prood as he wiz, streekit oot
afore no me but Me Enamourate –
thi grechtest ferly hereawa-aboot!

Eh'm thinkan, tho, that speerit wad abate,
be peerie-wearied frae ma fleesh, withoot
yir mercement – sae dinna brak oor date.

3

Gin Eh seemed ower thrawn, guid maister Cupit,
in effere ower derf tae be your serf,
yi ken withoot me scrievin here hoo erf
Eh wiz, aa guizerd up tae keep me dupit.

But noo Eh wull depone thi haill star-bag
is your's, frae core tae cosmos; naither Jove
nor ony thocht's mair puishant than is Luve,
nor Mars nor ony deed sall duck yir dag.

Lat this be kent by aa: thi burnin glack
Eh cerried in meh hert sic pleisures won
because uts codit swickirs she did brak

sae doucely; ilka jink she keeps undone.
Fur whilk Eh thank Luve, that wad peety tak
on sic as me; sae peety ivrywun!

2: *streekit:* stretched; *ferly:* marvel; *hereawa-aboot:* in these parts; *peerie-wearied:*
gradually diminished; *mercement:* mercy or discretion.
3: *thrawn:* obstinate; *effere:* appearance, behaviour; *derf:* recalcitrant; *erf:* shy,
reluctant; *guizerd:* masked; *depone:* make a formal statement; *puishant:* powerful;
dag: thrust; *glack:* puzzle; *swickirs:* deceitful moves; *doucely:* gently; *jink:* twist.

Morn-Come-Never

Sall ilka morn's licht hae this motherie
waurmth o yir *nganga* haunds that clap
aa glawnicies fae
ma body's een? That far countrie
o bairnhood that
we aa replace wi fear
becomes a bed.

This is thi glamir-gift, tae shift
time frae thi shouthirs o thi lift,
this brichtness o thi branchis shufflin cloods,
yir herr. Thi semm
renn skuds in us
as you muve, slamp ti conjerr
wi smoorikins an
yir fingirs' hurlochs
sic misgruggilment o miserie.

Eh feel yir sma haunds catch
up coonties in me, coup and
creel crans o aa thir datchie toons,
meh industrial hert,
Eh feel'um thring
this dunchit wean's crune
oot o me, lyk
ficklin wi a clarinet.

motherie: shell-like; *nganga:* (Zimbabwean) traditional midwife with mediumistic
and herbal skills; *glawnicies:* optical illusions caused by witchcraft; *glamir-gift:*
the talent to enchant; *lift:* sky; *skud:* to rain slightly; *slamp:* supple; *smoorikins:*
stolen kisses; *hurloch:* a falling or rolling mass; *misgruggilment:* rough handling;
coup and creel crans: entirely overturn; *datchie:* cunning, secret; *thring:* squeeze;
dunchit: tightly bundled; *crune:* a murmuring or menacing sound, like that made
by an angry bull; *ficklin:* doing something intricate that others cannot.

The Dominie

Thi cat's een gae
as silly-saft as luv
as tho tae pruve
hoo gleg-set yir ain's
blue gledge is, a
jonquil stapped in snaa.

I middie-fochtir o
seam an cyprin's splore
she loups oan thi bed,
a mense wee mockage
o this Bastet that beeks
i yir shoudirs' airch.

gleg-set: steady; *gledge:* stare; *stapped:* stuffed, rammed; *middie-fochtir:* mid-struggle; *seam, cyprin:* male and female sexual secretions; *splore:* antics, splash; *loups:* leaps; *mense:* gentle, shy; *mockage:* parody; *Bastet:* an Egyptian cat deity; *beeks:* appears suddenly.

Two Lyrics
(for Debbie)

1

Deid thrappils o fehv irises
still rax fur licht's yill
lyk mummifehd gorlins:
therr's a drouthy shill

til thir jaas that swaws thi lug
until a sweel o renn's
ahent ma broo, burnan oan yir panes
lyk a dirlir inna mill.

Air huds thir napes lyk
yir ain haund oan meh neck's back:
air's aingul taks up
oor herts' dinnil.

2

Dildirmoties o ma dreams
still seem tae dingil i yir een,
Etruscan, amygdaloid.
Meh hert wull lean

alang yir ribs lyk a gang-plank,
knockin wi thi ling
o meh luv's crew, that mak merk
here, anent thi sailin.

Thi chaumir's mumbudjit wi
sun: yir herr's leam's
hullockit, carn-tangilt wi
licht but we twa hae seen.

1: *thrappils:* throats; *rax:* reach; *yill:* ale; *gorlins:* fledglings; *drouthy:* thirsty; *shill:* a weak sound, as of wind (here used figuratively); *jaas:* jaws; *swaws:* disturbs; *sweel:* a rippling sound; *ahent ma broo:* behind my brow; *dirlir:* a vibrating stick that strikes the large bolter of a mill; *dinnil:* vibration.
2: *dildermoties:* difficulties that blind one to something; *dingil:* gather, resound; *ling:* tread; *mak merk:* sign on, make (their) mark; *anent:* re; *mumbudjit:* utterly hushed; *leam:* gleam; *hullockit:* wild, crazy; *carn-tangilt:* tangled like the roots of a tree.

The Landfish

than i sat doune to see the flouyng of the fame. quhar that i leukyt
far futht on the salt flude. there i beheld ane galiasse gayly grathit
for the veyr, byand fast at ane ankir, and hyr salis in hou. i herd
mony vordis amang the marynalis, bot i vist nocht quhat thai menit.
Yit i sal reherse and report ther crying and ther cal.

THE COMPLAYNT OF SCOTLAND

Wan mornin as Eh waulkd aside thi Tay
waatchin uts white hoarsis gae
in lings an brattils till thi spray
did seem tae extravaig entirely fae
aa bridlin o the currents: sae
ma thochts werr brangilt wi the brack
and ut seemd thi verra horseman's wurd
wiz breelin i thi swack
that coorgyit ma koarky-heid,
Eh saw an unca brachton cam
lidder speid tae shore.

Ut wiz a muckil boattul
in whilk a man wiz jammd
aa bowsie i thi bowfarts wi
fleesh lyk lubbertie,
lour-shouthirt wi a lurkit fiss
crammd i thi neck,
anely'iz hair free-flarin til
thi waatir's geck.

Eh loupit in an gunnilt him
an haald thi man ashore
an lookit furra soustir
tae mak thi man a door
ootfrae'iz glessy cell:

lings: lines, ropes; *brattles:* sudden rushes; *extravaig:* ramble, leave; *brangilt:* shaken, undermined; *brack:* brine; *horseman's word:* a secret word by which the initiate gains complete control over his horses; *breelin:* moving quickly and noisily; *swack:* heavy wave; *coorgyit:* hit as if to challenge; *koarky-heid:* light-mooded, feather-brained; *unca:* very, awfully, uncommonly; *brachton:* clumsy man or thing; *lidder speid:* at slow speed; *bowsie:* swollen; *i thi bowfarts:* unable to free oneself from a difficulty; *lubbertie:* jellyfish; *lour-shouthirt:* round-shouldered; *lurkit:* creased, folded; *geck:* play, trickery; *gunnilt:* caught by the gills; *soustir:* large stone.

he oped'iz een
an froze ma haund
as tho ut werr nae mair ma ain
than a spider i thi sand.

Hiz lips began tae fitch an flaff
hiz leths began tae fike,
a singir inna studio
that didna hae a mike;
Eh read whit he wiz speirin:
'Brither, say
whit land is this?'
an moothit back 'Thi Tay, Thi Tay.'

He loukd'iz lids
an lukeit as furdwabbilt as thi fleh
that sum aalmichty wabstir hiz
jist drunk dreh,
hiz lips werr lyk a fishin-line
that suddently gaes slack:
'Aweel, ma gawsie lad,' he sedd,
'jist throwe me back.'

Ut seemed Eh wizza boy again
that sciffies stanes as tho
he wad fill thi river,
be ut deep assut is wide,
Eh pickt up thi boattul an
flang ut it thi fiss o thi tide
then foond masel i thi waatir
spleuterin by'iz side,
an like a sailor tint at sea
Eh grabbd'um lyk a bride
an redd 'climb oan, ma gilpie,
Eh'm gigsman til yir ride.'

---

fitch: move restlessly; *flaff:* flutter; *leths:* joints of the fingers; *speirin:* asking; *loukd:* closed; *furdwabbilt:* very weak, enfeebled; *wabstir:* spider; *gawsie:* healthy, good-looking, plump; *sciffies:* flicks flat stones in order to make them skip across the water; *tint:* lost; *gilpie:* a lively youth; *gigsman:* man in charge of a winding engine in a mine.

We wur flochtin inna flim
that gleckt wi licht,
skellin oot a gleet wan meenut
an sookin ut up thi next,
an sae sappilty wi soond
that yi werr vext
wi thi sang aa roond
until yi cudna find thi beach
nor ken gif ut werr oot o reach,
sic a glag an glaibir
did thi waatir seem tae mak.

Tae stoap ma heid fae reelin
at thi sea's talk
Eh lukeit doon – an foond
ma freen's lips peelin
thi fouth o lagamachie
intae ae shanty:

veyra veyra   *veyra veyra*
gentil gallandis   *gentil gallandis*
veynde i see him   *veynde i see him*
pourbossa   *pourbossa*
hail al ande ane   *hail al and ane*
hail hym vp til vs   *hail hym vp til vs*
caupon caupona   *caupon caupona*
caupon hola   *caupon hola*
caupon holt   *caupon holt*
sarrabossa   *sarabossa*

As he sang Eh heard a crew repone
aa roond us, voices booncin thru
thi ice that bummelt up aboot us
lyk dumplins grinnin inna dolphin stew:

flim: haze; *gleckt:* flashed, played with; *gleet:* shine; *sappilty:* soaken; *glag:* gurgling or choking noise; *glaibir:* babble; *fouth:* abundance; *lagamachie:* rambling discourse; *repone:* reply; *bummelt:* boiled, bobbed.

kinkd: caught painfully; *bluachie:* bluish; *kinchd:* twisted; *gleg as Kilmaurs' whittlirs:* sharp as knives from the Ayrshire cutlery town; *skittlirs:* squirts.

          hou   hou
        pulpela   pulpela
        boulena   boulena
         darta   darta
    hard out steif   hard out steif
    afoir the vynd   afoir the vynd
        god send   god send
      fair vedthir   fair vedthir
       mony pricis   mony pricis
      god foir lend   god foir lend
          stou   stou
            mak fast and belay

Nou ut seemd wi stude upo thi deck
o a galleon aa kinkd up
i thi hert o a bluachie berg,
men kinchd an swam aboot thi shup
gleg as Kilmaurs' whittlirs
tendin thi raggity sheets o thi wreck
tae ordirs that cam lyk skittlirs
frae thir droonit skup:

             heisau   heisau
              vorsa   vorsa
               vou   vou
      ane lang draucht   ane lang draucht
        mair maucht   mair maucht
         yong blude   yong blude
         mair mude   mair mude
       false flasche   false flasche
          ly a bak   ly a bak
         lang suak   lang suak
         that that   that that
         thair thair   thair thair
        yallou hair   yallou hair
         hips bayr   hips bayr
         til hym al   til hym al
       viddefullis al   viddefullis al
       grit and smal   grit and smal
         ane and al   ane and al
          heisau   heisau
             nou mak fast the theyrs

Skey assa skeppie-bee, ma freend,
noo freed, did scamp aboot thi scob
o this ship, clamant assa claik
jist faan aff a tree in Buchan;
bellyhoolyin'iz fate
an beatin'iz bahoochan
intae sasiabilitie, thi mate,
fur sae he cried hisell,
did noo relate
this vessel's vagrin historie:

'Ut is thi whales' redargue
that we shid be redimit wi
this rimy wame, tae caa
oor ain craft's coronach,
be cliftie up hir clinkant masts.
Sacklessly we slew a skail,
laivin wan sanshach she-whale
oot o aa thae families
lyk stramlach oot ahent us.
She follyit thi wedow-path, stey
wi dool an doosht wi lorn,
that leads back til thi Tay,
wherein hir flanks werr torn
by coontliss canty brods.

Brochty men werr croose i thi craw
wi thir gebbies bricht lyk terns
till she clauchert i thi caochan
o'ur hert, spleuteran thir trews
an shoon, as the saga says,
makan Tay wan broth o'ur bluid
an fleean that murdirous pend

skey: frisky, spirited; *skeppie-bee:* honey-bee; *scamp:* wander mischievously about; *scob:* hollowed-out container; *clamant:* crying out; *claik:* barnacle goose; *belly-hoolyin:* bewailing; *bahoochan:* backside; *sasiabilitie:* state of satisfaction; *vagrin:* wandering; *redargue:* confutation of another's actions; *redimit:* crowned; *coronach:* lament; *cliftie:* nimble; *clinkant:* spangled; *sacklessly:* thoughtlessly; *skail:* school of whales; *sanshach:* cunning, evasive; *stramlach:* anything long and trailing, a rope or piece of dress; *stey:* obstinate; *dool:* grief; *doosht:* confused; *lorn:* love, desire; *canty:* active; *brods:* sharp instruments, spears; *Brochty men:* men from Broughty Ferry; *croose i thi craw:* full of self-confident talk; *gebbies:* mouths, beaks; *clauchert:* moved feebly about; *caochan:* stream; *pend:* lane (the Tay).

as faur's Stanehive
whaur she made an end
o thi music o that tribe.

We haald hir carcage back
hauf rottit, tae lair hir oan
thi common loan,
we made hir fleesh a shack
fur aa tae veesut fur saxpence,
a kinema o thairms.'

Gourdit in thon crystal ee
Eh saw thi wave's gilravage
Eh saw thi lang whale dee
lyk a wumman cut afore me
an crullit fae the savage
fiss o thi confessir:
'Whit has this tae dae wi me?'

'Dinna cum thi strangir, son,
Eh kent yir grecht-granfaithir
that brocht back a seal
an kept ut inna bath:
you sall be oor clangir, son,
a galshach furra gallan
cleidit up in ballan,
we sall assuage thi waatir's wrath
wi a singan meal.'

Blocherin wi grisky need, that crew
did claut at me wi haunds lyk croy
an claistir me wi blaubs o blubbir,
returnan tae thir weelkent labour
they did flense and jint me
intae lengths, jupein me thi while Eh'd be
thir slicin sassinger.

---

carcage: corpse; lair: bed or bury; loan: green; thairms: intestines; gourdit: contained, encased, bottled; gilravage: pillage; crullit: shrank; fiss: face; clangir: one who cleanses another of a wrong or disease; galshach: titbit; gallan: gallant; cleidit: clothed; ballan: baleen; singan: singing; blocherin: coughing with a gurgle; grisky: greedy; claut: clutch; flense: strip the blubber from a whale; jupein: mocking; sassinger: sausage.

As meh laggert banes
werr heistit owre thi side
thi mate preservd ma heid,
cryin ut by mony daffin names
as 'Tam-o-thi-speik'
an 'Billy Bunn,'
until thi wark wiz done.
An then, wi mony a groffy keckil,
he set ut oan thi gubirnackil,
declarin me this craft's kenspeckil,
until'iz tale wiz run.

'I thi keeroch o wir lust
whan we liftit wir whale
tae lig oan dust
by the strength o'ur tail,
hir jaw-hole gaped
and up she spewed
aa squeegeed up, a loit
maist glabbir-hued
wi kent wiz yet tung-shaped.'

Aabidy wiz dehvin owre thi side
whan thi mate gied me
wan last aside:
'Tay tuke thon,
left us squabashed
wi lips lyk stone
while she sings oan furivir,
an you, that own
a tung alone
o aa yir membirs' quivir,
be mindit oan
thi justice o this bond:
yir a dwaum o thi rivir.'

---

laggert: besmeared; *daffin:* licentious, joking; *groffy:* coarse; *gubirnackil:* helm; *keeroch:* awkward, sloppy work; *lig:* lie; *jaw-hole:* drain (here the mouth); *squee-geed:* misshapen; *loit:* mess; *glabbir:* filthy; *squabashed:* silenced; *dwaum:* dream.

Sae sings thi ootwalir, thi Jonah-jaas,
landit wi thi ee o thi maas
that ower-fret thi Tay,
landit wi thi lug o thi sailor
that didna plug oot thi play
o'ur cauld waatir sirens.
Eh see thi waves aa loupin wi banes,
skeleton-skails lyk harps in chains,
Eh hear thi strone o ribby strings:
fair taken by aw
wir falderal, Tay sings.

ootwalir: outcast, one who is left; *jaas:* jaws; *strone:* gush, spurt; *falderal:* fuss about trifles.

In *The Globe*, Dumfries

o the passenger
he rides and he rides and he rides
he sees things from under glass...
IGGY POP

Eh'm drinkan till thi *Globe* sterts birlan
waatchin you aneath yir gless fremms,
Burns. Repeatit doon thi waas,
aye keekan left as tho intae thi past.
Did John Keats cam here fur hiz furst dram
oan July furst, echteen echteen,
fresh frae yir mausoleum wi
his strange mude oan'um:
'anti-Grecian, anti-Charlemagnish'?
Sae Scoatlan still
wi 'cold Beauty' sall
confoondir fancy's wabbit will.
As Keats kent weel
anely thi haill dishabilment
o aa o reason's guizes wull
delivir truth.
       A human tooth
uncovert by a pleuch, thi pairt o a false gum
liggin plestic inna park, thi numb
haun clingan til a bridle, or
thi vakeit fiss
that's blinkan thru
thi broukit windie o a car
tint in Whitfield, Sanquhar or
Bellshill.
      This pub reminds me o
thi *Fisherman's* i thi Ferry, as tho
distendit inna dwaum. Ut
reels awa ayont thi waas
o thon bien howf as time speels
past thi glesses oan yir fisses, Burns, intae
that ae vacancy that wiz
within that ithir *Globe*, that spun
because o Shakespeare's tirlan wurds.

Thon hoop o naethin, thi nakeit roond
Eh traivel thru
(in brithirhood wi mair nor you:
wi mair nor mony sustren too)
wha's anely population is thi wurd.

Wiz that whit Keats thocht, goavan oan
thon mirliegrugous clood
o whirryin Dantean ghaists?
he hudnae kent thi cauld cud mak sae mony.

birlan: spinning; *wabbit:* feeble or exhausted; *dishabilment:* undressing; *pleuch:*
plough; *vakeit:* emptied; *broukit:* smeared, runny; *tint:* lost; *dwaum:* dream; *bien:*
comfortable, well-appointed; *ae:* one, same; *tirlan:* ringing; *mirliegrugous:* horribly
disorientating; *whirryin:* rapidly moving, driving off.

Hawthornden Morning Blues

The flehs buzz by meh windie
in the early mornin heat,
the flehs buzz by meh windie
at a hecht o thurty feet –
gif Eh wiz a fleh
Eh wadna daur tae fleh sae steep.

Eh'm sittan in a castle
that's sittan owre a greenwuid glen,
Eh'm sittan in a castle
that's sittan owre a growthie glen;
Eh've gote a man inside me
wha ut is Eh dinna ken.

The Esk slaps through the forest
lyk intirference oan a screen,
the Esk slaps through the forest
lyk trouble oan a TV screen –
therr's a wudwose in ma wurds, man,
Eh've aften heard but nivir seen.

Oh Lord therr is a spidir
and she's drinkan frae ma hert,
Oh Lord therr is a spidir
sookan bluid oot o ma hert;
gin you cud skelp that spidir
that wid shairly be a stert.

The flehs buzz by meh windie
lyk the thochts abune a heid,
the flehs buzz by meh windie
lyk thochts abune a schemin heid –
thae flehs that wad bide laicher
ur hingin in a wab or deid.

growthie: fertile; wudwose: wild man of the woods; skelp: strike; abune: above;
bide laicher: stay lower.

80

To a Fly

Sae, lacewing fleh,
when wull you deh,
an oor fae noo, or mair?
Yir jaiket's green
's the palest seen,
lyk leaf new helt ti air.

And yet the time
in which you climb
is no telt oanna watch;
ae meenit's span
can whiles expan
till airth utsel wad hatch.

That muckle fleh
wad crack the skeh,
gae fleein aff in space;
uts jaiket's hue
wad be bricht blue
tae no luke oot o place.

But in that deep
the oors they keep
ur nane that we cud dree:
oor sun can turn
and ithers burn,
that fleh sall nivir dee.

whiles: sometimes; *dree:* endure.

Fabula

(After the painting by El Greco in
the National Gallery of Scotland)

Ut's nivir a flemm
thon boy is blawin oan:
sae quhite
a licht.

Nor issut sum gemm
fur aa thi buck-toothit grin
o thi reid-cappit wan:
auld man monkey kens.

Th'embir lukes lyk breid
an breid that lichts a caunnil
can anely feed
thi hert.

Ut lukes lyk a rose
that gees instedd o needin
fire – sae blaw, laddie, blaw:
lat fire fill

thi petals o yir cuffs
an collar
rowld lyk foreskin, lyk labia:
blaw douce oan life.

An when yir braith fails
or yi puff ut oot
Gode hissel is blaan
wha faulds iz aa fae doot.

douce: gently, sweetly.

82

TICKA TICKA

Under all…forms and varieties of the external and internal man, still with hardly an exception, I have found him unhappy. With more capacity of enjoyment than any other creature, I have seen him surpassing the rest of existences only in suffering and crime. Why is this, and from whence? What master error, for some there must be, leads to results so fatal – so opposed to the apparent nature and promise of things? Long have I sought this error – this mainspring of human folly and human crime. I have traced through all their lengthened train of consequents and causes, human practice and human theory; I have threaded the labyrinth to its dark beginnings; I have found the first link in the chain of evil; I have found it – in all countries – among all tribes and tongues and nations; I have found it.

– from the last oration of EPICURUS
(in *A Few Days in Athens*, by Fanny Wright, 1813)

'A scab is a scab is a scab'

– a woman sacked from TIMEX
(speaking on Grampian TV, 14 December 1993)

A Temporal Ode

Time you make the angels grow threadbare,
you glue the skeleton's foot to the accelerator.
You advise me to drink less and make
my mind bend more like drastic polythene
when I take drugs. You prune my cranium
with tiny invisible secateurs
in order to gain cheap laughs.   ´
I, whose hairline once was as persistent
as the ancient forest of Caledonia.

You reduce my chances of appearing in the movies
by killing off John Cassavetes and Bill Douglas.
You make my friends' ambitions small and wrinkled
like a yellow rubber duck on a barbecue.
You remind me if I'm not part of a group
I'm part of an isolation.
You allow me to fill this space
with unrevised sheets of inked-up paper
from as many trees as once
crowned the pow of Scotland.

You cause me to anticipate
future sexual crankinesses
such as the fetishisation of tartan,
of seaweed, of fish and chips,
of tartan lycra, and women with glass feet.
You cause me to fear the popularisation
of my favourite lonely obsessions
with prawns, with Norman Wisdom,
with sculpture and bedside fittings made from seashells.

You cause me to doubt the realisation
of my schemes to reassemble the grassy cathedrals
of St Andrews, Balmerino and Arbroath.
To conduct there ceremonies of my own invention
which will cause you to yield up the past
in a gaudy theatrical regurgitation of
some Pictish poets, of Wang Wei and a half bottle
of rice wine, of the partly-digested manuscripts
of James Wedderburn, and as much of Frank O'Hara

as a jealous Heaven will release,
as even a timber wolf will do, if nuzzled
in the right place
by the right timber wolf cub.

Time you eater of forests and
of small fleshly computers, you
love us because we bought the gimmick of
eternity, and never turn our cars, never swim
for the riverbank: we run like a cat runs
when it isn't being chased,
but wants to think it is.

You love us because we keep putting
our weeks in the washer so they keep
getting smaller. Because we keep
believing you can sell us more
weeks, more angels, more forests.

Time you think we return your sentiments
but it's only cupboard love.
We did without you before and,
later, we will again.

Liberty Tree Dreaming

There is a great clock buried in the desert.
I know because I have been pushed
through the dirt onto its handless face.
There the spirits gather, walking the tracks between
the world's hours, the low roads.
I've been trying to trek back to Scotland
for nearly two hundred years, and am now,
the Wandjina tell me, at the Kimberleys.

I was Mealmaker, gatherer of men's rights,
weaver of radical thoughts into revolutionary action,
Secretary of the Friends of Liberty,
planter of the tree in '92
in the High Street of Dundee,
writer of the pamphlet condemning war with France

which got my friend, the Reverend Thomas Fysche Palmer,
transported. In all these years
I couldn't find him on the spirit tracks.
The Wandjina say he's ahead of me,
walking the ocean road home.
The ghost of William Pitt is trembling
in dread of his arrival.

I was Mealmaker, miller of the necessary grain
of justice and equality – that's all I can
remember of myself: to be
transported is to lose half your ghost or more,
caught in mindless shreds on the jails of Arbroath,
of Edinburgh Castle, Perth.
I remember the riots of '95:
rather than accept the pacifying bribe
of the Town Council's grain,
bestowed by their 'meal committee',
we tried to liberate our own
from the ships in the harbour.
I declared then, 'We ought to have had
a revolution long ago, and the present is
the properest time to have one.'
What is true is always with you;
what is worth your life is not forgotten.

I was Mealmaker, threader of secret pacts,
leader of the United Scotsmen of '97,
who campaigned for universal suffrage,
our own parliament, and I had dreams
of further freedoms, beyond money,
beyond wars, that I have sown
like appleseeds behind me in the desert.
The Wandjina say they can see
a great tree extending flat
along my route, its branches shaking
ghost leaflets about, shedding hope-fruit,
weaving water-of-life through many communities.

My trial took only three days, even though
young Davie Douglas wouldn't testify, and was
transported. They said I'd planned to burn
the jury's houses in a great bushfire
of seditious wrath. Not proven: I would

have burned far greater houses down
if I'd had time – of Parliament, of Hanover,
the banking houses and those of trade,
the houses of nobility as well as of
Dundee's nouveau riche. I would have left
a desert far barer than the one my spirit walked,
a scotched land in which everyone would
have had to fend for their own thoughts,
crawling on the blank clock-face of history.

Logantime

The seagod's arms held the clashing rocks
apart, like fingers between the bells
of an alarm clock, while the Argo sped
beneath, into myth's hourless world.

It was the New Year's Day movie in
Dave Logan's house and he was one
of the clan of uncles my father gave me
just by working in Timex: all

the children of sub-managers watched
the film whilst the parents of our
extended family got pished, picking food
up from a round tupperware dish

divided into hour-big triangles filled
with chipolatas, cheese cubes and pickled
onions on cocktail sticks, button biscuits.
We sipped cordials like little gods

as Jason drew his sword in terror
at the sowing of the Dragon's teeth,
the springing up of skeletons
that clacked their jaws and cut down

uncle after argonaut, advancing from
the eternal seventies into the slow
retreat from factory to factory,
the bony tick of recession's feet.

Keaton's Blues

One time I worked with this deafmute
and we just swept the factory floor,
smoked *Woodbines* in the toilets,
and that was where that summer went.

Gradually I stood up and walked into
his silence like Keaton walking through
the screen in *Sherlock Junior*, then
I didn't speak to the other students anymore.

One man who understood sign language
taught me that dancing alphabet, and
my friend hung over his shoulder,
nodding, showing me the tricks of hand

for anger, resignation, work and rest;
his intricate suggestion that we take
a fag-break. Both men gave time to show
that language is the ordinary dance.

Then the deafmute took me to
an empty loading bay, and pointed at
another factory. He showed me how
he had worked furnaces there,

the timing necessary to play
fire properly, then shrugged by way
of explanation for him working now
on this more menial level. The shrug

seemed fuller for stilling his
hands' dance, containing more
frustration, more of the way
the city tries resisting this slow

constriction of its industries.
I thought that one word filled
with such eloquence could reveal
a poetry behind our every gesture

returning with the flame and not
the throttled flower of Scotland, with
a music like revolution, before
the supervisor came and chased us out.

The Testament of Fanny Wright

1

I can see it all from Spring Grove Cincinnati
where like a cicada I lie in the earth
waiting for the year of my hope's rebirth.
I don't need to return to Miln's buildings, to
my Nethergate, to know the nature of the fight
at Timex, that was at Camperdown, that was
at Dunsinane Estate, at Milton of Craigie.
You don't remember what my father risked
for our cause; his profits from
the manufacture of thread for
the printing of *The Age of Reason*, his friends for
the Friends of Liberty. But then
his nerve was snipped with Palmer's arrest,
the hounding of Mealmaker. I can see
me being bundled into the rowing boat
in the deep silent dead of Dundee's night,
together with commemorative medals of Paine,
letters from Lafayette, even the book
he'd staked so much to hold.
I was a child, swaddled in the paperwork
of Revolution. He rowed from Craig Pier out
to the middle of that mile-wide outpouring
of Tay's chill sermon on
the futility of struggle
and threw the lot in.
I thought he would throw me too,
the baby with the babble of equality,
down to the dark phrontisteries
of crab and nibbled fisherman,
to argue that the tide would turn one day,
as though the hands of a clock went backwards,
disobeyed their master Time. To change
Tay's compassionless millennia,
its flushing away of all our bones of hope,
into a mind. But there he left me,
girl-Moses in the nodding boat,
while his figure, his resolve, shrank
towards America and died within a year.

2

What could I grow into but a virago,
and where could I crack the whip of my tongue
but in Dundee? My upbringing wrapped me in
the weavers' songs as in a sheet of newspaper:
I could hear nothing but men's voices
in the heckling shops and think
their wives should think thus too.

The hecklers had
such desire for news and information
that one would read aloud
while the others worked,
and so they argued and acted in combination,
like the pattern in a cloth.

But fatherless in the Scottish Geneva,
I could feel
each Dundee woman try
to rise in the Radicals' morning
from beneath the deadweight pages,
the dream-bibles pressing on
endlessly-issuing wombs.

Then, when I was eighteen,
my wrath thickened against this cult
that forced women down
to a lowlier posture than their striving men,
and, like a good Epicurean, I wrote
A Few Days in Athens,
my first assault
on the faith that undermines
freedom's reason.

But now, witnessing the world-wide game
of the same-minded masters,
and how my city's factories have changed
their gender and their product, but not their pains,
I see I must become its sybil, be
these managers' banshee, and like
my kirk-burned sister Grissel Jaffrey,
and that brief visitor,
the fieldfare Mary Shelley,

I must be
the third of Dundee's Eumenides.

3

From beneath this tree in Cincinnati
which my homopterous hope shall climb
in due course, in a transformative season,
let me disobey time; tell
my story backwards, crabwise, how-
soever will convey my urgent message.
For I have seen the revolutions fail
and far more than
one strike, one factory fall.

Having grown into a harridan, then
where should I crack the whip
of my soprano tongue next
but in America, where
my father's body sank through the dirt
into a shiftless grave?

I lashed the rocks of slavers' backs,
first with the rod of my rhetoric, then with
my father's wealth, which bought
negroes forth in families. Half-Moses,
half-matriarch, I led them from Memphis,
Tennessee, to two thousand acres
on the banks of Wolf River
which I called Nashoba.

Here I fell ill with a feverous dream
of their freedom and education
until this too sank
into a river of state legislature,
and they were taken from me to Haiti.

From this I learnt the owners may
not free the slaves, for they
themselves are shackled by their money
and the ways all nations shall permit
them to spend it.
None shall be free while there's a state
with which they must negotiate.

4

We all go down like father's papers
into the wetness of Tay's grave, bewailing how
it should have been. I know:
I've heard the others sobbing through
their coffins at
their funerals, but
most are silent soon enough.

They usually complain about their work,
their husbands, what
their children did not give them time to do.
These are the points passed through
by the minute hand
of the clock of our days.

I know: I married that feckless man
Phinquepal d'Aursmont
because he was a Pestalozzian
among other, baser motives:
a waxed moustache and a renown
which was, I later found,
self-circulated, and would have required
his waxing another part
to truthfully fulfil.

Most of all because I dreamed I'd found
another kind of man, part-mother, so
I could remain part-writer.
But Dale Owen was right, his 'wilfulness and
inordinate self-conceit
destroyed his usefulness' –
you forget so many of us were
in love with France itself.

In fact, you forget so many of us,
considering it is
we spirits who bewail a cause
who will not slip into the further depths;
we, who are concerned
with history's hours.
Forget our mapwork and you will keep
returning to the minutes' maze,

our lesser miseries
of income, childbirth and disease.

But while we were alive
our minds were minute-driven too,
I know, I confess.
Mine's was a fly upon a plate
who sees the swift slap come
and can escape;
its eyes are not constructed to observe
the slow-moving finger which
will stub it out.
Crushed beneath the intimacy of failure
I retreated to Cincinnati with my daughter,
there to die bewailing.

5

Women beware men with ethics in their mouths:
I have heard the sons of Calvin preach
outside the factory gates, raising themselves
above your distress, saying
'Either we shall all go back,
or the factory shall shut...'
and counting both a victory.
Such morals belong in the Presbytery:
who does such a principle punish? Those,
who like your former masters, have none?

'And not or'
was the only saw
the whole of my life could prove
a just law.
As Solomon with the baby, so
we should be
in choosing between
the minutes' decisions
and those of the hours.

My father was right to flee
so powerful a network of informers
as the Tories had established –
wrong to despair.
Mealmaker was wrong to stay,

but right to agitate until arrested,
right to hope beyond transportation
of a perfect society.
Who does such a principle sustain?
Those, who like your union men,
have not yet dreamed of it?

Remember we
are trapped upon a clock-face,
of which the arms are blades
approaching us
at differing speeds and heights:
what man can tell
which way to jump?

For one of these will catch us all
– scab, manager and worker –
We must at least learn to focus on
the slower, most inexorable one.

6

My mouth grows melancholy with the weight
of disappointments on it but
I will protest at your predestinarian
damnation of the scab.
I never found my freedom had a Hell
to which all enemies and fools
must be condemned,
though since my death I have seen
many slaughter many
as Grissel Jaffrey was burned
because of what men thought she thought.

My only commandment was
the secondary part
of that great paragraph: 'That
whenever any Form of Government
becomes destructive of these ends...'
(that is Life, that is Liberty, that is,
above all, the pursuit of happiness)
'...it is the Right of the people
to alter or abolish it, and to institute
New Government...'

– If anyone must preach at all
in order to be heard,
then let the lesson be:
break the system, not
another worker's head.

Therefore I uncoil my rauchle tongue again,
lashing these men as I would lash
their managers, since both
are cut from one economic cloth,
as once, in America,
I lashed evangelists:

'The victims of this odious experiment
on human credulity and nervous weakness
were largely women. Helpless age
was made a public spectacle,
innocent youth
was driven to raging insanity,
mothers and daughters carried lifeless
from the presence
of the ghostly expounders of damnation.
All ranks shared the contagion,
until the despair of Calvin's hell itself
seemed to have fallen on every heart
and discord to have taken
possession of every mansion.'

7

The age of believing in the music of the spheres
even though we cannot hear it
is over. That is what I thought
the revolution meant: the haar of glory
hitherto attached to kings, viscounts and
factory owners, had been dispelled,
a new angel had arrived
to sit in judgement on the Law Hill,
what Mary Shelley called
'the eyry of freedom'.
Now property should be abolished
and all should tremble equally before him.

Except, being male, he stumbled, and all
his feathers turned to papers

scattered on the waters, sinking.
Then, being male, his limbs came unstitched,
and fell quivering on the city and the river.
One arm destroyed a rail-bridge
I'd never seen be built,
and sent a train-full down.
Another limb wiped out the Overgate;
his skull rolled down the Hilltown
and bowled the Wellgate away,
and then his spine and ribs were taken
for a whale's, and hung
in a museum I never knew of
in Barrack Street.

And so we all were left bewailing in
our scattered graves, as union men began
bargaining within the system we had thought
destroyed; declaring null
our new republics, agreeing with their bosses
our further dreams of statelessness
were impossible
(even as their industries behaved
as though no nation was their home).

But in the depths I heard them, the drowned
in colloquy: gathering the feathers in
the sludge-filled carriages; discussing how
the change must scorch within,
how militant negotiation
is another name for war; stitching
my father's papers into a wing.

Where are their equals in the town?
Those who have gathered my own
forgotten words, and those
of my transported brothers,
my prophetic sisters?
Who is weaving the second wing,
the cicada cloud?
Who can hear the angel's fullest,
most hermaphrodite song:
'only the impossible is a just request,
those who merely demand
the reasonable shall always be denied.'

The Mothers

The QCs always called them 'girls',
just in case. If a female got married,
she floated round like a giggly gondola
beneath blown-up plastic finger-gloves,

their parodies of condoms. If a male did,
they'd leave him in his Y-fronts, tied
to a pillar in the canteen, covered in
shaving foam. Management was nearly

exempt, but never from their tongues,
which lashed across the social gap
men dreamed a bigger salary had opened up
and left authority around their ankles.

Graduates of engineering they checked out
against their own all-seeing skills
by showing two nearly non-existent tiny screws,
then asking for unneeded advice.

Small wonder that a student, male,
should walk among such women of
precision with averted eyes, smiling to
those on either side of him on the line,

then trip, and gouge his fingers open,
be frightened as they watched
him bleed, and be so comforted by
the care of so many mothers.

Praise of Italian Chip-shops

That summer, in a small glass booth,
I sat and set strapless watches
to within ten seconds of test time
all day, as the women did all year.

Fifty a tray times twenty trays
whilst trying to chat to Joe Capitelli
whose name kept sending me into
a dreamtime of Dundee shopfronts:

'Grilli', 'Piscini', 'Vissocchi'...
an ice-cream float of mock-Italian:
'Scella da peas on da coontah...'
here was another timelessness:

red mock-leathery booths of the cafés
in Blairgowrie and the Ferry,
yellow tartan formica of the chippers
in Stobswell and Arbroath.

The decor of my time machine was fixed
on sub-Art Deco forever, binding me
to Italy, binding the fifties to me on
a waft of milk-froth and lard.

Here I first perceived the rocket
machinery of coffee-propulsion;
the catholicity of a sugar-censer;
the madonna of the knickerbocker glory.

Here I first encountered the folded
pizza supper that would translate
as *calzone* in Florence; the two tiles
in the Spanish chippie in Blackness,

painted with tambourined dancers like
some pan-European Eve and Adam: all these
cleared me an hour from the cease-
less grasping hands of the clock

in which I could just sidle in
to the black marbled cool dimness
of Benni's on the corner of Corso Street
and buy time back in sliders.

Ticka Ticka Glendale

I was James Young Geddes, Whitmanic in Dundee,
calling vengeance down on Cox and Baxter,
inventing Glendale as their apogee,
the terrible Jute-Lord, revealing to my public
his crab-like face, he who could be
      man and factory at once;
a mausoleum-like amalgam, mounting the slopes
of the Law Hill, flexing his stalk-eyed clock-towers,
'Lit up at night, the discs flare like angry eyes
      in watchful supervision, impressing on the minds
      of the workers the necessity of improving
      the hours and minutes purchased
      by Glendale & Co.'
I did not flinch as he ate my fellows whole,
his smoke-claws waggling in the air,
his crab's arse excreting in the Lady Well.
His legs were the mastaba-tenements in which
they dwelt and died of TB, of cholera.
I thought he was Dundee's own monster, and
      would never leave
tormenting us with investment in his luxuries:
'The gardens and vineries of spacious extent;
The product, vegetable and fruits in their season.
Inside the house, case, culture, comfort, refinement,
Pictures, some of them Scriptural, *The Rich Man and Lazarus,*
      The Descent from the Cross, The Light of the World;
The Library well-stocked; Carlyle, Ruskin, Emerson, in evidence...'
But, battened on battle, spreading since Napoleon's defeat,
triumphing at the Crimea, feasting on the Civil War
in America, as a crab feasts on corpses, I saw
Glendale invest the profits of his jute abroad
      in Oregon, in Texas, in Hawaii.
I saw his devils roam the New World: the agent
Robert Fleming foil all my dreams of justice
by failing to catch the *Atlantic*, which sank
with six hundred lives off Nova Scotia,
surviving instead to purchase the Matador
Land & Cattle Company, which after years of profit
was bought out in 1951 for $20 million. I saw

the agent William 'Dundee' Reid go gold-baresark
in the capital-hungry farming communities
of the North-West, making 12% on loans
funded by fees paid by ordinary Dundonians
        (who saw nothing of the returns)
to solicitors investing in his schemes,
which included setting up rival companies
        on ever more imaginary
middens of capital. For this he earned
the dubious acknowledgement of Senator Nesmith:
'There are three liars in the State of Oregon
        and William Reid is two of them.'

Glendale, you let lunatics like Reid
build a bridge of paper across the Atlantic
by which you hoped to drive more profits into Dundee:
railroads slid off it at the first whiff
        of litigation over leases;
the first glut of Texian cattle and
the prices and your bridge collapsed.
Fleming fled to London like a wary matador
        and founded a merchant bank.
You invested in the wrong hemisphere
while Calcutta rose like a horseshoe crab,
obscuring your sun with sky-big bales of jute
sweeter than the whale-oil stink of Dundee's,
cheaper than your workers could be forced to produce.
You should have spurned us then, swam with
your factories on your back for India;
by failing to leave you failed, proved yourself
merely local, our bankrupt patriarch.
I saw you hiss out such bubbles of money
from your maw, bursting as you died.
I watched your carcase subside into the Tay
where the crabshell stank for decades.
The stench alone made me retreat to Alyth where
        I died too, my poetry obscured.

Then I saw a new vision
of the years succeeding my ignored eloquence:
from the waters came a swarm
of small crabs, mutated so
their claws were on their backs,

100

swivelling and searching out.
And the women of Dundee all slept upon the Stannergate,
and the crabs crawled onto their wrists,
and held fast.
And they began to feed on the subtlety
of the women's fingers, so that when they awoke
the crabs had sucked all the bones out from their hands,
and they could not lift their children
nor cook any meal
nor find any work.
Then I rushed through the streets in search
of another Glendale, a merchant of Dundee, anyone
who could say, as Gilroy said, on being asked
had he seen finer than Niagara Falls:
'Yes I have – 10 ½ oz/40 inch hessian coming over
     Gilroy's calendar at five pence a yard...'
someone with whom I could plead
as I had pled a hundred years before:
'Glendale! there is a spiritual law of supply and demand
     which is higher than the law of the economists:
The demand of that law is that your relationship with your
     workers shall be human and sympathetic.
You cannot get rid of your obligation by appealing to the
     necessity of securing cheap labour,
     to compete with the foreigner.'
But as I searched the fattened crabs
fell from the women's wrists
and I could find no one to talk to but
the innumerable clock-faces on the crabs' backs
as they sidled back into the waters of the Tay.

And then I saw that what I had prophesied
would happen in all parts of the world
had indeed come to pass:
'The native will give up his wooden gods, he will become as
     enlightened in matters of religion
     as David Livingstone;
For this you will give the native the blessings of
     civilisation – you will erect him slums like to those
     of the Overgate and Scouringburn;
The Slaver will no more carry away his children – they will
     be brought up on the half-time system;

He will no longer eat his enemies; he will consume the
      earnings of his children – the necessity for cheap labour
      unfortunately not allowing you to employ himself.'
But Glendale was extinct: his end abandoned us
to homeless scavengers; his genus had
mutated to invasive creatures,
no longer tied to one town as
the Sphinx to Thebes or
the Minotaur to Knossos,
but feasting where they would.
Then I understood there was no help for my people,
and I called out to them as they marched,
searching out their Glendale:
'You must destroy all parliaments, all kirks,
      all wages, all armies;
everything between you and these feeders.
You must fight the very system, not
your masters: for they are gone
into its further corners, and no longer recognise
the face or the hands of this town.'

But my tongue was wormy, and I could see
they roamed like flies beneath the glass
of a great clock-face,
and could not hear me.

Temporal ode
(slight return)

Time I try to keep you in check
by wearing a scratched old Snoopy watch
I made my father give me at fourteen
instead of his vast selection
of divers' watches which I imagined being worn
in the Deep Sea Restaurant in the Nethergate;
the watches with times of other countries
like America or Australia (did they show
Aztec calendars? could they tell
dreamtime?); watches with
the digital displays that Timex took
too long to cotton on to, thereby dooming
Dundee more than a decade ago;
watches that were radios, like something from
sixties' spy series we never realised at the time
were spoofs; space watches which gave
the times on different planets
according to their rotations around
distant suns; dinosaur watches, such as
pterodactyls wore on their ankles,
soaring on Permian thermals;
coroners' watches, which gave the times of death
of Lincoln, McKinley and JFK;
edible watches, available in mint
and juicy fruit flavours, which could still
be heard ticking, if you put your ear
to your friend's stomach; and of course
nuclear watches, which melted through
your wrist, but were accurate for aeons.

I chose the stupid Snoopy watch,
where the dog batters the tennis ball second
round in an impossible circle, with
the racquet in his minute hand,
flailing his hour arm. Often slow,
frequently stopped, as though time could
be gripped by tennis elbow,

I chose it because
I hoped you'd be ridiculed
into keeping your distance.

The perspex cracked, dust collected
beneath the plastic disc on which
the tennis ball was printed,
the strap broke. It took my father
two years to reassemble
the primitive technology necessary
to repair it, and then Timex closed.

Time you keep it ticking
on and on, attached to my wrist long after
I grew out of that phase;
it survives relationships, jobs, houses.
Time you prove to me that trash
can become precious, because it shows
our brittle workings can endure, the dream
of personality survive a little while.
Time you turn the dog's head to a skull,
you make my joke a penance to presumption,
you do not mind looking ridiculous
as long as one day you may eat me
as you will.

OMNEGADDRUMS

POEMS IN SCOTS:
1983-1991

FROM DUNDEE DOLDRUMS

2nd Doldrum
(Elephants' Graveyard)

Whaur ur yi Dundee? Whaur's yir Golem buriit?
Whaur doon yir pendies lurks it?
Broon brick, eldscoorit, timedustchoakit,
blin windies – whaur's MaGonnagal's hert?
Creh o seagulls echoes thru closies' lugs:
nithin but'iz hertsherds, shatterit, deidtrootdreh,
nithin but vishuns o lehburers deean.

Eh kent yi i thi street; Peddie Street
whaur boarn an raisd in tenements
ma sowelclert sheppit; Eh spoattit yi
certin a wheelbarra ower cobblies
(ower tarmaccadum and undir um's thi cobblestanes,
deid buriit jaabanes o yir weans' hopes),
Eh saw yiz in grey overalls, een deid an blank,
heid bulletgrey an taursmearit, durt
clung til yir een,
and indivisibul fae yir past,
oot o thi fremms o photygraphs
waulkin weldit tae wheelbarra,
haunds soldert tae toil, an nae rest.

Ghaist o thi Thurties, Dundee whan thi Daith cam doon,
grey cinders descendin, meldit wi claiths an dreams,
Dundee whan Amerika fell,
Dundee whan thi Depreshun cam owerseas
an bidit, an restit in oor faithirs' braces –
oor flatbunnits! oor bandylegs! oor rickets!
Waulkin uppa street, a deid, a ghostie,
a passedby, a damnit, a wurkir –
ghaist restless and nivir kennin green.

pendies: lanes; *eldscoorit:* scoured by age; *closies:* tenement entrances; *hertsherds:*
heart's shards; *deidtrootdreh:* dry as a dead trout; *sowelclert:* soulclay; *weans:* child-
ren; *taursmearit:* tar-smeared; *bidit:* stayed, remained.

10th Doldrum

(Arcades)

Gnaa, then; rent! these yir bowels, yir moniplies,
these yir hollowit hallowit caverns –
Arcades, Ark, *et in Arcadia ego* –
ego, te morituri...ach!
Whaur's thi stinks, thi noise, thi chuckies burnin,
Bar-B-Cue, gowden driplick, bastit, birlin:
whaur's thi café, durty linoleum, green tiles;
coaffy plasticmuggit, hamburgirs in floory rolls,
whaur's thi machines, machines; penny Arcade;
Logroll, pennydrappit, broon Britannias, boabs an tannirs?
      Aa gone, aa wede awa.
Nae lichts skinklan, thi clash gaen roon,
an me a wean, scuttlan in atween thir knees,
crabfishent owre thi flair;
men pleyin pool, pleyin pinbaa;
clash, crash, cavern hole – smell o fush,
      sellin toys an toaffy aippuls:
bizzy wame, undirgroon, by thi men's bogs;
stew o piss an clang! auld voices,
an noo thi haill thing's abaysit, nithin:
jist graffito
           WEERABOYZECKDAVIDSUNSHED
– Runes, echoes, dowdybroon, broon o Ameriky:
broon color o wastit dwaums, diners, durt;
broon o sleep, haurd fisses in loam;
crackclack echo o deid Dundee voices –

Dundee, yi Gollum! yi Prometheus!
Whit yearns o commerce tore yir entrails oot,
whit scrawny hoodies hing owre yi?
Puir affwhite boady nivir i thi sun afore,
tidemarks o durt cleggit roon yir neck an ahent yir lugholes,

wha's blaan thru yir belly lyk a dose o sauts?

moniplies: entrails; *birlin:* whirling; *skinklan:* glittering; *clash:* talk, gossip; *abaysit:*
confounded, ill-treated; *crack:* witticism; *yearns:* eagles; *hoodies:* hooded crows;
cleggit: stuck, clotted.

NOTE: The Arcades were market stands formerly found beneath the Caird Hall.

11th Doldrum

(Auld Leddies)

These auld hae tint thir men and time;
auld wummen, clochecappit, fat,
layirs an layirs o ancient undirwear;
sit doon, alane, ankliesswole, readin:
Romance, Nursis' Luv, D.C. Thomson Times —
mappamundi o a tapewurm; smell o pee,
innards whinge wi age, blethirs quake.
Auld leddies, wi Raadio Twa, wi kirk ootins,
wi Mystry Tours roon thi cornir,
wi fushnchups an dreid o Pakis,
wi lumpen High Teas, bellies fou wi scones,
auld leddies wha've furgoattin hoo tae pray,
auld leddies, lament fur ye:
                              ach, yi bags!
Auld leddies, jittrin inanootae butchirs' shoaps —
twa poark choaps fur yir week,
lamb's livir fur yir tank o a spaniel;
Penshun queue oan Thursdays,
gashin tae auld leddies an nin o yi lissnin,
nin o yi kin even undirstaun thi ithir onymair:
auld leddies sendin wee lettirs sans punctuaishun,
sans grammar, sans news:
                              sendin wee lettirs
tae ithir auld leddies, tint in Brechin, Cupar;
auld leddies lingran decades eftir hubbie deed,
auld leddies dinna ken thi streets namore,
dinna ken thi shoaps, dinna ken thirsels,
auld leddies lingran bloatit shepps o Dundee past:

lament fur yi as yi greet in yir lanely hames —
        yi bunch o daft Torie coos!

11th Doldrum: *tint:* lost; *mappamundi:* world picture; *kirk:* church; *gashin:* gossiping.

22nd Doldrum: *wurmin pangs:* hunger pains; *doon-haddirs:* suppressors; *doddy-mittens:* fingerless gloves; *pintil:* penis.

NOTE: Winter's print McGonagal's work; the poet lived in Paton's Lane; he was "awarded" the Order of the White Elephant.

22nd Doldrum
(White Elephant)

MaGonnagal yi nivir thocht tae question why
that Philistine crew
                    kept you,
lyk thi souvenir seal packt up fae thi Arctic
in thi tin bath o thir affecktaishun;
tearin aff
            ivry wance inna while
    anithir strip o blubbir
tae fling tae yir neeburs wi
thir wurmin pangs:

        yi thocht yi werr
thi veritable whale o genius
oan a mission up thi Tay
            tae mak Dundee TT
fur Queen Vic & auld leddies ivrywhaur.

Yi Goliath amid gairdinless gnomes,
yi Samson that geed clippins awa
tae thae doon-haddirs, Delilahs in doddy-mittens
        an wad-be Noarth Britonians, Winters
        thi Printirs;
did yi no ken hoo they needit you
tae pruve therr wiz nae poetry
    in poverty, in prostitushun, in Patons Lane?
        – an sae nae cause fur ackshun.

Yir crucifyin neeburs
thocht yi werr thi vast irrelevance,
used yir verse
                tae wipe thir erse;
gied you thi last lauch o impotence,
peyed you this compliment thru
thir ain incompetence:

white elephant seal oan Calvary, thi Law:
quaartirs o yir boady hing
fae Balgay! thi Mercat Cross! fae Reres!
Fule that maks a haill toon fuleish;
you link poetry til thi warkirs sure's
thi pintil's linkit tae thi wumb!

King of the Green

A slatir fell
frae thi clints o ma broo
thi scrogs o ma herr
an craad aboot ma buke,

a forkietaily tickilt ma lug
an keekit oot
an nibbilt oan ma eardrum
ridan up therr,

a gollowa flew
awa frae ma glower:
Eh sall be thi King o thi Green
an nane sall me withstaun!

---

green: park, drying area; *slatir:* woodlouse; *clints:* cliffs; *scrogs:* bushes; *forkietaily:*
earwig; *keekit:* peeked; *gollowa:* ladybird.

The Mother

By thi time Eh gote therr
aabidy wiz fleean –
we'd aa been doon thi *Shup*
since we gote ootae skail
cos ut wiz open aadey.

Well, he wiz staunin by
thi recordpleyir wi
a fag anna gless and
Jimmy sez, he sez EH TUKE
A BLUEY EH TUKE

A BLUEY and he sez
Eh've gote sum stuff, dyi waant
tae cum wi me? Well, Eh
wiz haufoan masel and
he's fell guidlukein, ken.

Eh sez Eh wiznae oan
thi Pill – he's rowlin wan
o thae things an he sez
yi can suck ma cock then.
Well, Eh widnae dae THON!

fleean: drunk; *haufoan:* nearly drunk.

The Derelict Birth

Fit barnie fur yir bairnie-haein?
– Therr's nane
i thi Inane
      wi thi mune fur a midwife,
      bricks fur a crib.

Nae meddum kent o frankincense.
Th'Immense
maun hud thi mense,
      but thi mune's yir midwife,
      ash his bib.

Coco-de-Mer

Dinna bathir wi thi braiggil o wir lends
that maks a cothaman o gravy
i thi cot, but famine in wir crullit herts –
let gae oan thi dumbswaul, be
brankie i thi breakirs, an flocht,
flocht lyk thi crospunk intae Lewis –
thi lucky-bean tae thi haunds o thi misk.

The Derelict Birth: *fit:* what; *meddum:* tickle in the nose, portending a visitor; *maun:* must; *mense:* gentle.

Coco-de-Mer: *braiggil:* a dangerously unstable article; *lends:* loins; *cothaman:* surfeit; *crullit:* cowering; *dumbswaul:* a long, noiseless sea-swell in calm, windless weather; *brankie:* pranked-up, ready for fun; *crospunk, coco-de-mer:* the Molucca bean, drifted to the shores of some of the Western Islands; *misk:* land covered in coarse, moorish grasses.

Grout and Pamisample

Ane nicht, faur frae the seafront,
pawmrin owre thi hungry-groond atween
the lampies lyk a palissade in negative,
papplan oan thi heckle-pins
o exile frae aa purpose-fu acts,
an laithin thi keek-me o sang oan masel,
Eh stoappd, an niffert wi thi nicht,
paleit thi caundils o thi leerie-lichts
'Whit wey shid Eh be gaean in ma hert?'

Eh saw inside ootfrae the sile o ma mind
a billatory rise, aa bowdens in
thi gosky gress. An whaur thi een
shid be, Picasso's jet in curlin daurk,
twa nichthawks did Eh see, faibil
white oan gallus luchts, and whaur
thi nostrils nichthawks, and aa
ut mooth mumbudjit wi moth:
ile-grout oan shore. Grout an pamisample.

grout: any oily evil-smelling remains; *pamisample:* the shell Bulla lignaria; *pawm-rin:* going shabbily and idly from place to place; *hungry-groond:* ground credited to be so much enchanted that a person passing over it would faint if they did not use something to support nature; *papplan:* tumbling, boiling, perspiring; *oan thi heckle-pins:* in a state of uncomfortably suppressed expectation; *niffert:* bartered; *paleit thi caundils:* demand of a death-candle whose demise it indicates; *billatory:* a restless uncontrollable bull; *bowdens:* swollen with wrath or over-eating; *gosky:* rank, coarse, feeble; *nichthawks:* large white moths often seen on hedges in summer; *gallus:* wild; *mumbudjit:* silenced.

The Gairfish

At first sight, it would be thought beneficial to the salmon fishing, if a method could be invented, by which the porpoises, or Gairfish as they are called, which devour so many salmon, might be destroyed.
— P. Monifieth, Forfars. Statist. Acc., xiii. 493

Lyk a selkie or an ottir wad ye be,
takin a glammach frae thon fozie saumon
    that wad cam back tae Scoatlan?
Ach porpy, bricht sea-pollock, ye shid ken
thi bourgeois winnae staun fur that;
    selkith can he see ablow
thi seaweed, seemin-solid, risin inna promontory
that tae thi tide's tug shufts; here thi gairfish gaes –
shooin thi waatir's brim in carefu slytes
    that laive aa boats ahent:
yir thochtliss scrift.
    Selkith can thi bourgeois hear
yir screnoch seep atween thi crancrums
o thi drivin seas –
              Aa he kens is sum buggir's et
    his saumonses, and's tint th'orts.

    'But,' (he sez), 'Thi gairfush nivir biggit aucht,
nivir scrieved a sang...'
(Nor did thi Homeridai till
Peisistratos saw thi gree)
    'Thi gairfush nivir foond th'ile...'
(Or nivir let oan, gin they did) –
    Thi gairfush pollutit nary an ocean,
    thi gairfush nivir inventit thi Boamb,
    thi gairfush nivir profitit fae onywan's lehbur,

gairfish: porpoise (the word is peculiar to the vicinity of Dundee); *selkie:* seal (believed by the Gaelic peoples to be capable of human form); *glammach:* a snapped-up morsel; *fozie:* dull-witted; *porpy, sea pollock:* names for the porpoise; *selkith:* seldom; *shooin:* sewing; *slytes:* smooth sharp movements; *scrifts:* fluent improvisations; *screnoch:* shrill cry; *crancrums:* things difficult to understand (here, figuratively, the currents); *tint:* lost, left; *orts:* what is left of food after the best has been extracted; *biggit:* build; *scrieved:* wrote.

114

'Therefore,
      therefore...'

But aye til them that tak thi doon-drag oan;
them that dallow i thi doggerlone o Poetese,
    ploutir amang sejoinit wurds;
        yi gleesh ayont th'offskep,
sloom ablow thi mairchent's gaff –
Aye yi seem tae them thon gairfush Arion rade,
baith ploongan and ascendan
i thi dance o sunlicht aff yir freithy plumashe –
        An thi splores fae'iz despirate mooth,
        singan fur dear life!

Gee th'ogertfou yir Giaconda's smickir,
gink at thi *Courier*'s unca-richt rant;
doistir oot thi Bummir's caas
    wi whut we'd cry a Socialist sang:
      'Here i thi sea
      we tak as we need
      an gee whitsoivir
      we hae tae gee.'
– That'll shak'um i thir baffies! That'll
threip thir panloaf mugs
intil thir tabnabs!

O meenisters & meenisters' wives, auld leddies ivrywhaur,
Jutelairds' ghaists & thi faceless face
    that "rins" wir deean facktries
                – Here's a force
    that nivir dosses, swimman in thir sleep;
a dab haund at cullin prickirs tae.
Here's a waukindreme tae mak yi girle:

doon-drag: the incumbent weight of a sin or a disgrace to a family; *doggerlone:* wreck; *ploutir:* splash heavily; *sejoinit:* disjuncted; *gleesh:* burn with a hard, steady flame; *offskep:* the utmost boundary of a landscape; *sloom:* move slowly and silently; *plumashe:* plume of feathers (here, figuratively, foam); *splores:* drops of saliva ejected whilst speaking (or singing); *ogertfou:* drunk with a sense of one's own good taste; *smickir:* grin; *gink:* titter to oneself; *The Courier:* local Dundee paper, owned by D.C. Thomsons, a somewhat conservative organisation; *unca-richt:* self-satisfied; *doistir oot:* drown out; *Bummirs:* factory hooters; *baffies:* slippers; *threip:* thrust; *panloaf:* snobbish, affected; *tabnabs:* tea-things; *Jutelairds:* those who made their fortunes from Dundee's jute mills; *dosses:* snoozes, is lazy; *prickirs:* basking sharks; *girle:* having one's teeth set on edge.

a skail o gairfush, omnegaddrums,
wi a thoosan makars oan thir backs,
snoovin up thi Tay thiday,
sall raise a sang lyk smirr tae faa
upo the wurkirs' polly-shees
an gar thum hyne yiz aa awa!
Thir plisky spit sall gar yi think
thi daith-dive's rinnin frae yir lugs
an drippan frae yir toaffy-nebs!

An this sall be a smore-thow
upo yir bourgeois pow –
luke up: ut's faain NOW !

On the Cold Lido

Gaubertie-shells at shore
an children lauchin oan
thi daurk esplanade.

Th'auld wuid steps
i thi middle o thi strand
fur divin when thi tide

is in. Splintirs i ma back,
Eh lukeit doon frae ma starry childhood
oan hur kaid.

The Gairfish: *skail:* both a school and a storm; *omnegaddrums:* a miscellaneous collection, a medley, the unincorporated craftsman of the burgh; *snoovin:* sliding easily; *smirr:* fine rain; *polly-shee:* a pulley attached to an outside pole, from which a rope runs to a tenement window, for hanging clothes to dry (another word peculiar to Dundee); *gar:* make; *hyne:* hoist; *plisky:* tricky; *daith-dive:* putrid moisture from a dead body's orifices; *smorethow:* heavy fall of snow that threatens to smother; *pow:* forehead.

On the Cold Lido: *gaubertie-shells:* a hobgoblin supposed to combine loud roaring with barking like little dogs, also the sound of shells striking against each other; *kaid:* used of cats, the desire for the male.

Scotland the Twit

Thi furst o things that Eh did see
oan Christmas Dey i thi moarnin
wiz Iggy Poap oan Brekfist TV
sing *Real Wild Child (Wild Ane)*
lyk a mental cat
that rowls i thi sun: aa
thi kiddies clappt, an Eh kent
ma brithir-eedjit, Osterberg, in thee.

Ma dreams furgoat, Eh tuke thi doag
oot, an saw a hoodie craw
pile intae a cauld auld poke
an hoap-awa-cassidy, an back, as we
went by, an Eh saw burds
peopul thi lawn's piazzas,
an ducks an peewits i thi waatir,
craws an gulls i thi throat o thi Tay
oan Christmas Dey i thi moarnin.

Thi sun'ud yet tae clear
a grecht clood carvit ower Fife
lyk thi warild's collar-bane,
an thi Tay's foil cairpet wiz
cream-coappir-gowd, seal-siller-grey,
suckan back lyk a wheen o fleas' knees;
Eh saw ut wi
MaGonnagal's sib ee.

Eh went tae thi end o thi pier
tae waatch fur seals, an sedd
'Affoard me noo ae vishun:
a dauphin bairn cleavin thi reamin
waves o thi Tay wull you
sit doon!' (this tae thi doag);
a flinty arraheid
o burds went by, as gif ti sey
'Wu'll hae nin o that noansinse.'

poke: chip-bag; *sib:* brotherly.
NOTE: Iggy Pop's "real" name is James Osterberg.

An whan thi sun cemm up
an Dundee cam alist in clementines
an neuralgia wiz bestowit oan me,
three swans Eh saw gae sailin by, twa siller
yin grey, oan Christmas Day...
an rejeckit thum
oot o haund; ut widna dae
tae seek ayont thi things
Eh'd keekit thru, save fur this paitturn's sake.

Beaker Man

(This skeleton is exhibited in Dundee Museum)

Yirth wiz owre waarm tae wauken'um;
noo he's bared lyk breid, an aeon's auldirs.
Banes dreh as whalirs' tack
tak color fae thi clart
as meh skin micht fae thi sun
eftir a lang hasky saturaishun.

Thi geegaw o fleesh seems fuleish
aside'iz ribs' splent bangils,
thi jiggirs o lorn in ma veens
gurthie an garish
by thi shaddas lyk pebbils
i thi lunkirts o'iz een.

Whit giff-gaffs cud fankil thi tendons
o sic sandman's fingirbanes?
thochts in thon skull'd be
dreh oats inna beakir,
an whit luves werr cradilt in
thon pelvic arc ur foondirt noo in saund.

Scotland the Twit: *cam alist:* respired.

Beaker Man: *yirth:* earth; *auldirs:* stale bread and pastries, sold cheaply; *clart:* earth; *hasky:* dry-throated; *geegaw:* decoration; *splent:* split, scattered; *jiggirs:* small, insistent pulses; *lorn:* desire; *gurthie:* corpulent; *lunkirts:* temporary shelters; *giff-gaffs:* interplay, give and take.

A Backlook

(to my father)

Presleyan, yi didnae waant
    ti be a tigir
rinnan aflemm thru gloaman
    o tenements
hittin thir tap-note o grey,
Sportan Post ticht-furlit in
yir haund.
        Uncranglan lyk
a quiff, i thi glistiry room
     whaur men ur biddubil.

gloaman: early evening; *uncranglan:* uncurling, relaxing; *glistiry:* hot, sweaty, flickering with light; *buddubil:* cowed, obedient.

The Socialist Manifesto for East Balgillo

I thi hovie an thi howd o sleep,
whaur Dundee dovirs oan thi rink
o ma frore-thocht lyk a Michael-
angelo oan skates, inna sowff o
faain, Eh gae back intae mains
oan mains o gorse an Pict-banes
whaur thi doozie-land's a roidit
rist, and Sandy Hole Gaelic's pirn's
unspoolan i thi prisk guschet
o aa thocht's birth's biforrows,

an therr, whaur garrons o thi speak
ur growein back lyk a lizard's tail
an aa'uts baists ur scarts an jenny-
wullocks, an aathin's lyk pellack,
thi peltin-pyock o aa "feel"osophy,
Eh pense o naethin, lat naethin be,
see thi mense o Scoatlan lyk Mozart's
gartillin concerto, hiz piana spaldit
assa smokie, and innuts paums
a gaitherin o chestnuts lyk shut een.

hovie: swelling; *howd:* swaying; *to dovir:* to be half asleep; *sowff:* murmur, sigh, doze, thought; *mains:* farmlands; *doozie:* flame (as of a candle); *roidit:* roughly made, not well finished; *rist:* stringed intrument; *pirn:* spool; *prisk:* ancient; *guschet:* corner of land; *biforrow:* before; *garron:* a small, sturdy horse, or an old, worn-out horse; *thi speak:* the talk, the language; *scarts, jenny-wullocks:* hermaphrodites; *pellack:* the flesh of the porpoise; *peltin-pyock:* shabby garment, suitable for rough work; *pense:* think; *mense:* gentle, meek; *gartillin:* great; *spaldit:* sprawled, split.

NOTE: Sandy Hole Gaelic is a kind of Double Dutch spoken in the part of Broughty Ferry where one of my grandfathers was born; similar "local" languages occur elsewhere in Scotland.

Keelie's Een

Wha can thole thi keelie's een
that kens thi waatir's curlicues
and ilka barleypickle i thi Carse
while ut tacks uts fethirs' sail
    an jidges thi whiddin hares?

Aa's but mirligoes he views
wha aince huz sic a glower in-seen;
stigmatized by aa's spurmuiks
thi warld's cauld jag is inniz veen,
    Ginnungagap gees sook.

Aberlemno Stone

Yince Eh'd seen atween thi groond Eh tread
an thon rouch stane thi Pecht'd raisd in yore
wiz a licht years' linn that laivit him
feet cauld inna ghaist o frore;
an thocht skewlit apert thru abysms
whaur Yird abandont Homer tae,
thi constellaishuns o blinradyous hopes
chinklin agley:
Eh bent heid til thi serpintwark,
threadit sang back thru thi centirless daurk.

Keelie's Een: *keelie:* hawk, also aggressive urban male; *barleypickle:* topmost grain on an ear of barley; *Carse:* the Carse of Gowrie, the river plain north of the Tay between Dundee and Perth; *whiddin:* moving quickly and noiselessly in a zigzag fashion; *mirligoes:* specks that dance before the eyes; *spurmuiks:* particles; *Ginnungagap:* in Norse mythology, the void before the world was formed.

Aberlemno Stone: *Pecht:* Pict; *linn:* stream; *frore:* frost; *skewlit:* deflected from the plumb-line; *Yird:* Earth; *blinradyous:* blindly-shining; *agley:* off the straight.

Pier's Pilgrimage

Ur yi wi me fears?
Wur wi yi Piers.

Ur yi by meh side, daith?
Eh'm by yir left side as aye.

Ur yi draain near, yi ancient bards?
Wur follyin yi, an thi path is haurd.

Ur yi roond me, luve, yi canny bee?
Eh'm hoavrin by, gin you cud see.

Ur yi near meh hert?
Feel meh smert.

Is ma wey thru peopul yet?
Thru thum, an thru.

Whan sall ma pilgrimage be din?
Whan aa o us yi sall ootrin.

FROM **ANITHER MUSIC**

Mappamundi

Eh've wurkt oot a poetic map o thi warld.

Vass tracts o land ur penntit reid tae shaw
Englan kens naethin aboot um. Ireland's
bin shuftit tae London, whaur
oafficis o thi Poetry Sock occupeh fehv
squerr mile. Seamus Heaney occupehs three
o thon. Th'anerly ithir bits in Britain
ur Oaxfurd an Hull. Scoatlan, Thi Pool,
an Huddersfield, ur cut ti cuttilbanes in
America, which issa grecht big burdcage wi
a tartan rug owre ut, tae shaw
Roabirt Lowell. Chile disnae exist.
Argentina's bin beat. Hungary and Russia
haena visas. Africa's editid doon ti
a column in *Poetry Verruca*,
whaur Okigbo's gote thi ghaist
o Roy Campbill hingin owre um. Thi Faur East's
faan aff – aa but China: thon's renemmed
Ezra Poond an pit in thi croncit cage.
France disna get a luke-in:
accoardin tae Geoffrey Hill, plucky wee
Charles Péguy is wrasslin wi
this big deid parrot caad 'Surrealism' fur
thi throne o Absinthe Sorbet.

In this scenario Eh'm a bittern stoarm aff Ulm.

One Priceless Shawl

'I have caught a glimpse of the seamless garment
And am blind to all else for evermore.'
HUGH MacDIARMID

Thi Dighty Burn haufchenns Dundee
past Clavirhoose tae Monifieth;
Victoria's Jutelairds birlt thir mills
upoan uts weelwarkt string, and still,
tho stapped oan irin, fermirs' dung,
ut dreebuls forth lyk woundit sang.

Eh pleyd aside uts droonin-doors,
thi jugular breenge o'uts weirs;
flang doon thi Seevun Airches' gulf
soustirs thru uts tree-tilet ruif:
against delicht in ut Eh tempir
thi coardit Tay tae whilk ut's hemp.

An metir, rhyme, these stanzas, prose;
aa meh feelosophic brose,
meh poem-products fur oor time,
tho backd up by thi deid's guid nemm,
ur like this slawpollutit burn
by that fur whilk meh peopul yearn.

But partial brenns exalt thi past,
MacDiarmit's brockenspectir's cast
owre aa, an cast again, till nocht
is seen o recent rinnin thocht
that waants tae weave a sang fae blackent
weed, rustit bike, but canna slacken.

Considrin hoo thi capitalist
demandit a price that couldnae exist
fur this wee burn's *haecceitas*:
ut turnt'iz wheels fur free, thru grace;
this mercatabil universe's
true foarm is value's big converse.

birlt: turned; *stapped:* filled to overflowing; *breenge:* rush; *soustirs:* large stones;
whilk: which; *brose:* pabulum.

An tak wurds frae thi dictionair
thir ainly sense's whit we share,
thir deep suggestiuns jist thi powl
tae ithir wurds: wan priceless shawl
shid be thi peopul's element
an poets' stoattin by dementia.

Knocked down

Evelyn Peenie pleyed i thi street
wi a doag caad Teenie
wi thi bark o a meanie
anna fiss that she thocht dead sweet
until, by thi licht o thi mune
she gote rin doon
by a bizzy taxi fleet.

I thi coabbils she fell on
she split lyk a melon
but a melon wi smergh an twa een,
but sicna a fiss
wad anely haud grace
furra Gode wi Picasso's een.

One Priceless Shawl: *stoattin:* staggering.
Knocked Down: *smergh:* brains, marrow.

Classical whispers

Whit dae they show us, thae
wha hae little or naethin tae show:
Lysippus, Calamis, Apelles,
Parhassius, Mentor, Mys,
Phidias and Praxiteles?
Noo an then they whuspir, noo an then.

Whit can we hear o them
whas wark naebiddy kens noo:
Cornificius, Bibaculus, Ticidas,
Caecilius, Calvus, Cinna,
whas scrannels widna plug a lug?
Noo an then they whuspir, noo an then.

We arena breathin fur
thi toomity stane
that faas aroond
some feenisht flame,
an skulls dinna suit a laurel croon:
bettir luvd noo nor i thi groond.

Talking Water Blues

(for Duncan Glen)

Well Eh went tae ma jaabox thi ithir dey,
Eh turnd oan ma tap an Eh heard ut sey:
'Eh ain't no waatir an Eh ain't no wine
Eh'm-a ZED TWO OH and Eh'm-a feelin fine!'
Well Eh powrd me a gless o this chatty bree
and ut sclimmd owre thi rim and ut sedd tae me:
'Yi'd better no scell me oan yir flair,
yi'll hae talkin lino and a talkin chair!'

    Eh've gote thi talkin waatir, talkin waatir blues
        (oobie-doo-wa, ba-oobie-doo-wa)
    ut disnae quench yir thirst
    but ye sure catch up wi thi news
        (oobie-doo-wa, ba-oobie-doo-wa)
    ut disna taste that guid tae drink
    but man, whit a liquid tae think,
    talkin waatir, talkin waatir blues.

Well Eh tuke wan sip an Eh stertit tae jaa
an since that dey Eh've nivir stoappd ataa,
ut's-a ZED TWO OH frae thi Planet Zog
whaur evrythin talks, man, tree and doag.
Well wance you let this stuff in yir mooth,
ye waant tae tell a leh but ut comes oot thi truth,
yeah, ut lukes sae douce as ut sits i thi gless
but whan ut hits yir heid ye jist huvtae confess

    Eh've gote thi talkin waatir, talkin waatir blues
        (oobie-doo-wa, ba-oobie-doo-wa)
    ut disnae quench yir thirst
    but ye sure catch up wi thi news
        (oobie-doo-wa, ba-oobie-doo-wa)
    ut disnae help yir flooirs tae grow
    but you shid hear thae daffies go man go,
    talkin waatir, talkin waatir blues.

Well Eh medd a pote o tea fur meh auld gran
an she spleutirt oot 'Wha geed this til a MAN?'
and Eh powrd an eggcup i thi River Tay
and ut skraikd that lood thi Noarth Sea backed away.
Well Eh set up shoap sellin ZED TWO OH
but that talkin waatir hud wan no-no:
'Yi can sell me by thi boattul yi can sell me by thi can,
but yi canna sell me til an Englishman!'

    Eh've gote thi talkin waatir, talkin waatir blues
        (oobie-doo-wa, ba-oobie-doo-wa)
    ut disnae quench yir thirst
    but ye sure catch up with thi news
        (oobie-doo-wa, ba-oobie-doo-wa)
    Eh've gote thi talkin waatir, talkin waatir blues,
    talkin waatir, talkin waatir blues
        (an that's news).

jaabox: large sink; *bree:* brew; *sclimmd:* climbed; *scell:* spill; *douce:* gentle, harmless; *skraikd:* screeched.